DREAM SPEAK

**Understanding The Hidden Language
Of Your Dreams**

MARK GOWLAND

Prima Materia Publications
www.primamateriapublications.com

Dream Speak
Understanding The Hidden Language of Your Dreams

A book about how to interpret and understand dreams
the way a depth psychologist would.

Copyright © 2022 by Mark Gowland

All rights reserved. No portion of this book may be reproduced in any form without permission from the publisher, except as permitted by U.S. copyright law. For permissions contact:

Prima Materia Publications

Cover Design and Layout by Robert Scozari - robert@scozzari.ca
Cover Illustration by Noreink

Book Illustrations by Scott Luxon - sluxon@gmail.com

First Edition
ISBN 978-1-7781208-0-0
All Rights Reserved

For my family

Acknowledgements

It always takes a village, no matter what. This book has definitely taken a small village. It has depended on some of the most intelligent minds over the past century to share their ideas, which have contributed meaningfully to this book. Most importantly, the genesis of this book could have not have been possible without the incredible work of Carl G. Jung, Marie-Louise von Franz and the people who have become analysts and built upon Jung's findings.

I spent a lot of time, money and energy poring through the the Analyst lectures from Jung Chicago. Especially helpful was the information gracefully shared by Robert Moore, Murray Stein, Lois Khan, Donald Kalsched, Jean Shinoda Bolen, Julia Jewett, and Thomas Patrick Lavin. I would especially like to thank the work of the intelligent analysts who taught me about the Animus. I could only rationalize what it could be when I was taught by a woman. I had to go to them to learn, because it was important for me to get it right, rather than to understand the Animus only from a man's perspective.

I would also like to acknowledge the work of Emma Jung. Her book helped me understand the Animus even more.

I would like to thank my Medicine Teachers: Erik and Nilda, Don Carlitos, Don Fernando, Don Alejandro and Old Hands.

During the Covid lockdown, I read Robert Johnson's book "Inner Work" and this was the inspiration to write my first book. Mary Ann Mattoon's book "Understanding Dreams" helped me go deeper.

On a personal level, I'd like to thank Robert Scozzari with Inspiring Design for helping with the design of this book, Scott Luxon for the illustrations, Chris Hampton for the editing, and my analyst CJB for all her help understanding my process, my wounds, my shadow, my Anima, and my Self.

For all everybody has done to make this book happen, thank you.

Introduction

> *"Dreams are messages from the deep."*
> — *Dune*

Although civilizations change and our experience evolves over time, humans are dreamers. The messages and visions we experience while sleeping instil a sense of awe, wonder, and power in our personal lives, as well within our collective society.

In 2500 BC, about 4,500 years ago, the first dream to be transcribed was carved into stone. The dreamer was the Sumerian King Dumuzi of Uruk, who ruled just before Gilgamesh. The surreal experience and the magical language of the dream spurred King Dumuzi to talk about it. Indeed, the incident was important enough to have it transcribed. The impulse is easy to understand: if we have a powerful dream, we feel compelled to talk about it. It is fascinating, however, to know that the dream maker speaks in a timeless language that is as relevant today as it was in the time of Dumuzi.

Here is the king's dream:

"A dream! My sister, listen to my dream: Rushes are torn out for me; rushes keep growing for me. A single growing reed shakes its head for me. A twin reed, one is removed from me. Tall trees in the forest are uprooted by themselves for me. Water is poured over my pure hearth. The bottom of my pure churn drops away. My pure drinking cup is torn down from the peg where it hung. My shepherd's crook has disappeared from me. An eagle seizes a lamb from the sheepfold. A falcon catches a sparrow on the reed fence. My goats drag their lapis lazuli beards in the dust for me. My male sheep scratch the earth with thick legs for me. The churn lies on its side, no milk is poured. The cup lies on its side; Dumuzi lives no more. The sheepfold is given to the winds."[1]

Can you remember your first dream? Which dreams do you remember? Our dreams have captivated, confused, enchanted, moved, shaken, and especially changed us. They have aided humanity in times of need, helped us make breakthrough discoveries, predicted the future, and inspired creative masterpieces. They are our greatest personal ally while we move from the cradle to the grave.

I cannot imagine a world without dreams. A world without a direct link to the great mystery would be impossible to comprehend.

Even the word "dream" has a special resonance in our society. The sense of potential contained by the idea is perhaps the reason why Dr. Martin Luther King Jr.'s "I have a dream" speech is regarded as one of the most influential speeches in human history.

In almost every religious text and practice, there is a mention of dreams. Most of the religious reform movements in Judaism, Christianity, Islam, Hinduism, Buddhism, (and many others) began with a practice of communal dream sharing.[2] Jacob had a dream of a ladder, Egyptian pharaohs had dream interpreters, Buddhists believe that the Buddha in training will have the same dreams as other Buddhas, and Aboriginal Australians believe that life emerged from the dreaming. Dreams have been at the centre of historical and cultural shifts and they are an important axis to a greater sense of being.

Not only have dreams been at the centre of how our mythological, religious and personal beliefs have shaped our world, but they have also made major contribution in the areas of business, art, and science. One night, while Dmitri Mendeleev was dreaming, he saw all the table of elements

---

[1] Alster, 1972, pp. 55 - 57; Wolkstein & Kramer, 1983, pp. 75 – 76

[2] jeremytaylor.com/dream_work/dreams_and_dreaming_in_world_religion/index.html

fall into place. It was in a dream that Einstein saw cows jumping back from an electric fence in a wavelike pattern, which helped him to discover his famous Theory of Relativity. Larry Page, the founder of Google, dreamt that he could download the entire web onto some computers. After doing the math, he discovered that it could be done, so he started Google. The famous surrealist artist Salvador Dali called his paintings "hand-painted dream photographs." His technique was that he would lie on a couch holding a spoon that was attached to a cup, when he would fall asleep, he would have a glimpse of the dream, and the spoon falling into the cup would wake him up and he would quickly sketch what he saw and make his art.[3]

I wrote this book as part of my dharma, my work in the world. It has been something that I could not help but do. I have benefitted so much from my dreamwork that I wanted to share it with people. Writing this book, has helped me learn so much more about dreamwork as well as myself in the process. I hope you do, too.

The book has been separated by key components that would make up dreamwork.

The 4-Step Process - The method is a process of using a first principles approach to dissect the dream into its many different symbols, then using these symbols to discover how they interconnect as a story. This is how depth psychologists interpret dreams.

The Archetypes - Archetypes are a powerful part of all of our unconscious. This part will go into what they are, how they show up in dreams, and how they show up in your life.

Types Of Dreams - This will explain some common types of dreams and dream symbols and elaborate on their meaning.

Dreaming Exercises - This section will explain different exercises to work with a dream to receive clarity on its meaning.

---

[3] https://www.bedguru.co.uk/9-inventions-inspired-by-dreams

Dream Herbs - This section will cover different herbs from around the world that have aided in dream work and their

Bringing Awareness - This is for when your dream journal is complete. They are introspective exercises to help you understand.

Dreamwork is quite an intensive process, and there is a lot to learn. I did the best I could to simplify this. Dream Speak is by no means a complete work — this is an introduction for the enthusiast. It would serve as a good beginner's guide to Jungian dreamwork, which is a practice that's vast and involved, but also most fascinating. The real work of dream interpretation is an alchemical process. The alchemists believed that the process of transforming lead into gold happened in seven stages, which also worked within a four-part process. Dream work is about your process of individuation, a journey to wholeness. It is about understanding your persona, making friends with your shadow, wedding your contrasexual archetype, and discovering your Self. If you are really serious about this, it is best to work with a Jungian Analyst (advice that I will mention a few times throughout this book).

There are volumes upon volumes of text just from a Jungian perspective about dreamwork. For some suggestions, check the bibliography. This book stands on the shoulders of giants, and for their investigations into the phenomenon of the psyche, I am eternally grateful.

I became fascinated by dreams at a very early age. Whether it was because of trauma, a need to escape, a creative impulse or a mystical intent, I am not exactly sure. I used to write them out as short stories for writing assignments as a young boy. It wasn't until I was 29, when I had my first session with a Jungian Analyst that I finally understood what dreams actually were.

I told my analyst a dream about an unknown "friend" of mine (a shadow figure), who has been dismembered by a butcher and given to me as a gift. I was concerned that this dream was more violent, or had some negative connotations, until she said:

"Why do you think he was cut up? Tell me about his personality."

"Well," I said, giving it a moment's pause, "I guess he was untrustworthy."

"I would say then that your psyche is killing off the part of you that is untrustworthy," she responded.

Something clicked. My mind was blown. I had never really understood that dreams were actually me, all my secrets, all my fears, all my energy, happening inside me without me even knowing! I had always thought that they were mostly just movies that I watched or experienced while I slept. It was at this moment that the shoe had dropped — dreams are me, they are the psychic underpinnings of my life, they are my "dark side of the moon." When my analyst had told me this, something moved, and I was hooked.

The real value of dreamwork comes from consistent and repetitive work. Writing down the dreams, identifying and interpreting the symbols, highlighting potent messages, meditation and contemplation of the characters, etc. That is where the growth is. Dreams are you; they are the real unconscious process that is happening underneath your daily life. By making friends with your unconscious, you will no longer feel like something is missing. You will begin to feel the effects of wholeness, and your life will become richer and more authentic because of it. Never mind reading self help books, read your own dream journals, and solve the great mystery that is your life!

I hope you get some benefit from this book. I truly do. I hope that you learn from it, and get the value that I did from writing it. I hope that your dreamwork assists in your awakening and individuation process. I hope that this book sparks an interest in turning inward and serves as a companion and guidebook for you on that journey. Most importantly, I hope that you have a really enjoyable experience reading this.

Alchemical Seal

Index

Introduction To Dream Speak   13

What is Dream Speak 13
Why Learn Dreamwork 15
Carl Jung's Dreaming Hypothesis 15
Reasons To Interpret Dreams 15
How To Use Dream Speak 16
Carl Jung's Map Of The Psyche 18
Term Sheet 19

4 Step Process   20

The Method 20
Step 1: Amplify Each Dream Symbol 21
Step 2: Connect To Your Inner World 23
Step 3: Find The Correct Interpretation 26
Step 4: Create A Ritual For The Dream 29
Format For Interpretation 31
Interpreting The Dream 34
Increase Your Dream Recall 39

The Archetypes   41

The Dream Ego 43
The Persona 46
The Shadow 48
The Contrasexual Archetype 52
The Anima 54
The Animus 59
The Self 63

Types of Dreams 67

Big Dreams 67
Little Dreams 67
Dream Series 68
Death & Destruction 68
Homoerotic 69
Repetitive Dreams 69
Nightmares 69
Numbers In Dreams 70
Colors In Dreams 70
Highly Emotional Characters 71
Children 71
Animals 72
Mythological Motifs 72
Protector/Persecutor 73

Dreaming Amplifications 75

10 Dreams 75
Getting To Know Your Inner Dream Community 75
Your Inner Animals 76
Dream Ego 76
Your Persona 77
Discover Your Shadow 77
Meet Your Anima/Animus 78
Lucid Dreaming 80
Create Something From The Dream 80
Using Dreams To Solve Problems 81
The Movie Theatre 81
The Bodies Dreaming 81
Chakra Dreaming 83
Dream Gestalt Exercise 84
Start A Dream Group 85

Dream Herbs — 87

Calea Zacatechichi 88
Silene Undulata 89
Mugwort 90

Bringing Awareness To Your Process — 93

10 Dreams Exercise 95
Inner Dream Community 96
Inner Animals 103
Inner Landscapes 110
Dream Ego 117
Your Persona 124
Discover Your Shadow 132
Meet Your Anima/Animus 139
Your Process 147

A Final Word — 149

Bibliography — 151

Man and Woman kneeling before a furnace where a transformation is about to take place.

> "...at the source of the dream there is a creative mystery which we cannot rationally explain.
> It's the creativity of nature. It's the same creativity which has created what man could never invent..."
>
> — Marie-Louise Von Franz:
> The Way Of The Dream.

The Sequence of Stages in The Alchemical Process

Introduction To Dream Speak

*"The Cave You Fear To Enter,
Holds The Treasure You Seek"*
– Joseph Campbell

What is Dream Speak?

I am sure you have purchased this book because there is a deep yearning, a calling perhaps, to venture into parts unknown within yourself. You are working with the archetype of the Magus and need to know more.

Because of this, you have been self-initiated into an apprenticeship with the Dream Maker. By working with your dreams, you will learn to navigate life by your own star. You will find your way through life and not live out the repeating mythologies of your past or ancestors. By learning to dream, you will find your way, guided by your inner star.

Learning how to work with your dreams, is learning how to work with your inner voice. Dreaming is natural. We dream every night.

The quest for your Holy Grail has begun just by having this book in your possession. Keep it secret, and keep it safe. Every knight who went in pursuit of the Holy Grail and followed a path made by somebody else went altogether astray.

By working with the Dream Maker and learning Dream Speak, your way will emerge. You will live a life meant for you and you alone. Dream maker will speak to you and give you advice meant only for you.

When you go to sleep, bits and pieces of your treasure map will reveal themselves to you in your dreams each night. Your life's quest will be uncovered by recording the hints and learning to decipher the sacred symbols given to you by the Dream Maker. The great mysteries of life will begin to reveal themselves to you, and the path that was once hidden will appear before you.

Dreamwork will not lead you astray but guide you home. Dreamwork will not disconnect you but deepen your connection to life. Dreamwork will not leave you confused but provide you with the light of clarity. However, dreamwork does not do the work for you. It provides you with the opportunity, but you and your conscious mind have to put in the effort to transform and build the relationship with the dreaming. You and the Dream Maker become co-creators in your life. It is your life and yours alone. What will you make of it? How will you live it?

Dream Speak is a translation workbook that records and explains the relationship between you and the Dream Maker. Dreamwork is a powerful and sacred process. It is best to find a Jungian analyst to work with for those who are serious about this work. Dreamwork is personal work, it is transformational work, and it is dynamite material. In our ancestors' old days, working with a wizard, a shaman, an oracle, or a priestess would help them transform. You, too, will need to seek out your shaman or priestess. In this day and age, they will come in the form of a Jungian analyst. Since this is a Jungian method, it is best to seek out and work with a trained Jungian analyst if this way clicks in with you. The rewards will be worth their weight in gold.

In mythology, it's the deepest and most frightening cave to enter that holds all the gold. Guarded by the dragon, you must learn to slay your inner dragons and seize the hidden gold that is rightfully yours. Now that you know this, will you continue with the work? Or will you live the rest of your life without owning your dreaming power? Dream Speak will help you find that.

So Why Learn Dreamwork?

Dreams foretell change, long before the change.

Learning how to dream gives the power back to you. It spurs you to live from the inside out and not from the outside in; you will take guidance from the deepest and most authentic part of yourself. You will reclaim your true dreaming power that lies within, and learn how to manage the tension of the opposites between the inner voice and the outside world.

Learning to dream puts you in the driver's seat of your own life. You will stand steady in your decisions and create a strong foundation within. With all this confusion in the world, we are looking for guidance and stability from our news networks, our leaders, artists, friends, and family — everybody but ourselves, the one person we should be listening to most. Dreamwork changes that.

By learning to understand your dreams, you take the power back in your life, and you empower yourself. You receive gifts and advice from your inner mentor, your inner healer. You become an apprentice of the Dream Maker, and your work is to live your most authentic life possible.

Carl Jung's Dreaming Hypothesis

- Every dream has meaning.
- Dreams add something vital to one's daily life.

Reasons To Interpret Dreams

- Dreams give you direct access to your hidden thoughts, feelings, and wishes.
- Dreams provide you insight into your psyche's situation as it is right now.
- Dreams operate without the filter of your Ego.
- Dreamwork accelerates your psychic healing process.

- Dreamwork grants you access to the inner conflicts holding you back.
- Dreamwork will provide you with the work necessary to become whole (your individuation process).
- They explain conscious attitudes you may not fully understand.

How To Use Dream Speak

This book intends to help you become whole and your own person. It has been created to strengthen the connection between yourself and your unconscious.

- When you wake up in the morning, write out as much of the dream as you can remember in your Dream Journal. Highlight, draw, or underline anything you think is important, and make notes about the Dream in your journal.
- Write all your dreams in your Dream Journal and make sure to be on the lookout for archetypes and the mythological motifs explored in the dream themes and following chapters.
- Work with some of the exercises on starting on page 93 to deepen your dreamwork.
- For every ten dreams, use the 10 Dream Exercise found on page 94.
- Once the journal is complete, make sure to use the other follow-up worksheets at the back, which include: Finding The Complex page 95, Inner Dream Community page 96, Inner Animals page 103, Inner Landscapes page 110, Dream Ego page 117, Your Persona page 124, Discovering Your Shadow page 132, Anima/Animus page 139, and Your Process page 147.

These amplifications are essential because they shine a light and help you understand what is going on behind the scenes in your everyday waking life.

It is to your benefit to work with a Jungian analyst as well. They are highly trained individuals that can help you through this deep and powerful work.

> *"Nobody has been initiated into the great mysteries and transformed alone. There were always helpers."*
> — *Robert Moore.*

Jung's Map Of the Psyche

Jung's Model of the Psyche

Term Sheet

Conscious: The awareness of your thoughts, memories, feelings, sensations, and environment. If you can describe what you are feeling in words, it is part of your consciousness.

Unconscious: The part of the mind that is not accessible to your conscious mind and strongly influences your behaviour and emotions.

Dream: The psyche's attempt to communicate important messages to the dreamer. Dreams are the psyche's process of developing the personality, which is the process of individuation.

Projection: Unconsciously using unwanted emotions or traits that you don't like about yourself or secretly wish you could be and associate them with somebody else.

Ego: The rational and realistic part of your consciousness. It is concerned with pleasure and can create a strategy to achieve this goal without jeopardizing society's ethical or moral code.

Amplification: To make dream characters, symbols, and emotions more immense, more significant, or more potent in your psyche by using personal, mythical, historical, or cultural parallels with the dream symbol.

Association: create a mental connection between a dream character or symbol to personal events, experiences, emotions, or mental states.

Archetype: Ancient and deep-seated forms of human knowledge passed down from our ancestors. They are universal inborn models of behavior and people that play a role in influencing human behavior and cultures.

Complex: Core patterns of emotions, memories and perceptions.

4 Step Process

The Method

Calcination

Before we get into exercises and dream characters, we need to understand how to record and work with dreams correctly.

Without a method and a systematic step-by-step process to understand the language of your dream, it will be a challenge to open up a dialogue with your psyche.

Things to remember when writing down your dream:

- Once you wake up, keep your eyes closed and review as much of the dream as you can, to remember it better.
- It is best to record it once you get out of bed.
- Do not look at your phone upon waking; it will wipe out a lot of your dream memory.
- Include the date.
- Make a note about how you are feeling when you wake up.
- Give your dream a title.
- Note any songs that were in your head when you woke up.
- Write out as much as you can remember, in as much detail as you can remember. Try to include what actions made you feel a certain way in the dream.
- Try to draw an image or symbol from the dream.
- Highlight or underline things you think are essential.
- For every ten dreams, use the Find The Complex worksheet on page 94.

Step 1: Amplify Each Dream Symbol

Symbolism is the language of magic.

After you have written out your dream, it is time to amplifying your symbols. Take each symbol (character, object, place, etc.) you see in that dream and make associations. What words, feelings, memories, or thoughts spring up from your unconscious? Start from beginning to end. Doing this will release and uncover the emotional energies that are within each symbol.

Make a list of each setting, symbol, person, color, object, number, and anything else that makes up the dream. Then start to make associations with them. You can play with the associations as well by using the examples of associations below.

Dream Associations

Personal: Personal associations you have with the dream symbol/image.

Community Swimming Pool — Swimming lessons, swimming lengths, boring places, places of pain, and fitness. Something my mother made me do. A sterile place for fishing. Water can represent the subconscious.

Relational: How the symbols relate to you.

Community Swimming Pool - I would spend many summers at outdoor community swimming pools getting swimming lessons. I love to swim, and have many positive memories with outdoor swimming pools.

Pop-up: Spontaneous instances that come up that you may have never even thought of.

Community Swimming Pool - I once got heat stroke falling asleep under a tree at the pool, there was a creek by the pool I would go to with my dog and she would swim around in it.

Collective: myth/archetypal associations explained on page 72.

Community Swimming Pool - Hero and Leander. Hero was a Greek woman and a priestess of Aphrodite who dwelt in a tower on the opposite side of a straight. Every night Leander would swim across the straight to spend time with her guided by the light of a lamp that Hero would light to guide his way. They are not allowed to proceed with their love by the gods or the overbearing parents, but Hero finally allows Leander to make love to her and they have a summer of love between them. One night, Aphrodite becomes angry with the two of them and she creates a storm when Leander is swimming across the channel large waves rise, and the lamp is blown out. He eventually drowns and dies. Hero by her own sorry casts herself into the sea and drowns as well.

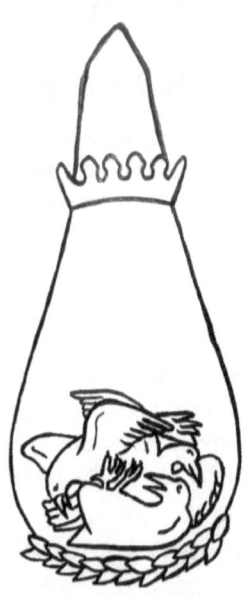

Dissolution

You don't usually need to go into this great detail, but if you are stuck on a symbol, these are examples to go deeper into the symbol until it clicks in.

In this step, you must break all the aspects of the dream down and separate them, like taking apart a radio to see how it works and finding out what each part is and means. In the next steps, we put it back together.

It is also important not to make associations about the associations because this can run amok, and we are looking for associations to the dream characters, symbols, and images only.

Step 2: Connect To Your Inner World

"The dream is the theatre where the dreamer is at once scene, actor, prompter, stage manager, author, audience, and critic."
— Carl Jung, General Aspects of Dream Psychology (1928)

Always begin your dream work with the practice of inward application.

Understand that the dream represents something that is going on internally within you and not externally. Start from there The Dream Maker tends to use dramatic structure and over-dramatizes dreams to help you remember them better.

Make Note Of The Dramatic Structure Setting: The most important place to start. Understanding the setting and how it psychologically relates to you will tell you what your dream could mean. A good question to ask about the setting is: "Who does it belong to?" The answer will tell you whose influence you're under or whose "turf" you're on. It could be your own, that of an archetype, or something else altogether. Trust that whatever comes up is what your unconscious wants to tell you. What emotional associations do you have with the setting?

Structure: How is the story of the dream organized? What are the significant elements?

Exposition: What is the background information within the story or narrative? This information can be about the setting, the characters' backstories, prior plot events, historical context, etc.

Protagonist: Who are the leading or main characters of the dream?

Antagonist: Who are the characters that actively oppose or are hostile to someone or something?

Plot development: What is the initial situation that propels the dream forward?

The culmination of the dream: What is the pivotal event of the Dream?

Lysis: What is the ending or outcome of the dream? How did it end? Positively? Negatively? Where is the psyche moving to?

Question: How does the dramatic structure relate to you and your life?

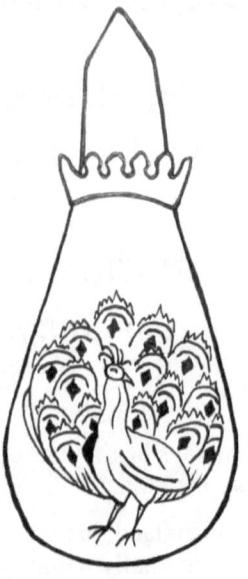

Fermentation

Connect your associations and symbols from Step 1 and weave them into a story. See how your associations and emotions connect through a dramatic structure. When you go back and look at the dream again and see how the associations and emotions you made from Step 1 fit into a story.

Do any themes relate to what is going on in your life?

Are you in a place of transition in your life? Does the dream communicate anything about this?

Does the dream seem to contradict the beliefs of your waking conscious? If so, in what ways?

What is your situation in life currently?

Amplifications

Amplification involves the use of mythic, cultural and historical similarities pertaining to the dream symbol. It means turning up the volume on cloudy dream symbols and uncovering or unpacking the bigger energy powering the dream symbol and the dream. Can you find any myths, cultural or historical similarities that relate to your dream symbol? (i.e., looking for a cup, could be searching for a grail. Meeting an old man under the sea could be meeting Poseidon) Primarily, how can we amplify or unpack the dream symbols to hit home in the here and now?

Associations

Associations give dream symbols personal meaning. You can begin by asking yourself, what are your personal associations to the dream symbol (people, objects, colors, numbers, animals, etc.)? What are some (if any) personal associations, feelings, ideas that you have in regards to the dream symbol? What you are looking for is gossip-type associations that are not necessarily politically correct, but how do you actually feel with regards to these dream symbols?

The Dream Series

Look at your past dreams and see if there are any repetitive or connecting themes relevant to the current dream you are interpreting. Does one dream you had a week ago set up a continuing narrative to this current dream?

Relational Questions

How does the dream relate to your life and your current conscious situation? How does it connect to your complex (core pattern of emotions, memories & perceptions), your dream series, and your life's present and future potential?

Once you have gone through Step 1 and connected the associations in Step 2, answer the questions and start to form your hypothesis about what the Dream Maker is trying to tell you.

It helps go back and use the dream structure with the associations rather than just the symbols.

Step 3: Find The Correct Interpretation

The dream is a source of information about the conditions of your nature that are relatively unknown to you, and it concerns aspects of yourself in which you have much to learn.

When approaching the interpretation, nothing can be assumed, and you must avoid all assumptions of the dream's meaning. You must trust that the dream will reveal its intentions to you. The Dream is not a disguise and also cannot be taken literally.

Seperation

You will have to accept that a particular person's dream image will bear some characteristics of yourself at some level.

Things to Remember

- The dream is not a disguise but a set of psychic facts.
- The dream will not tell you what to do.
- Find out what the dream is satisfying by conflicting, changing, or confirming your current conscious situation.
- Be aware of your personality and how the dream applies to you.
- What are your previous complexes, and how are they being presented in the dream?

Things To Consider
- What kind of emotions, stories, and feelings are in your conscious situation right now?
- What is going on in your life at this very moment?
- What happened in the previous dreams that are concerning this current one?

Important Factors
- What conscious attitudes does the dream conceal or offset?
- What is the complex or problem that the dream is concerned about?

Interpretation Aids
- The interpretation is usually something that you didn't know about yourself or are just barely aware of.
- The interpretation that inflates your Ego or is self-congratulatory is not the correct one.
- The interpretation that shifts responsibility away from yourself is not the correct one.
- Fitting the meaning of dreams into your life's long-term flow will help you transform in unimaginable and unique ways.

Other Questions To Ask When Interpreting

Most important question: How does this relate to me and my current life situation?

- What is the primary meaning that this dream has for my life?
- Why? What for?
- When I let the image come up, what comes up with it?
- What does this concretely mean for me?
- What does this have to do with me and my life?
- What sort of feelings did you have when you woke up?

- If you were to gossip about the dream character, what would you say about them?
- What is the emotional impact of the dream?
- What song was in my head when I woke up?
- Play with the associations
- What type of personal associations do you have to this dream interpretation?
- How do you relate to this dream?
- What "Pops-Up" for you when working with this dream?
- Collective (Myth/Archetypal) Are there any types of mythologies that could be associated with this dream?

Statements To Finish If Stuck
- The dream makes me feel…
- The dream reminds me of…
- The dream might be about…
- I hope the dream does not mean…

How to Verify The Interpretation

Ask yourself these questions:

- Does the interpretation connect with you?
- Does the dream interpretation "click in" with you? Does something move around in your psyche that elicits a particular "ahhh" response? That is what "clicking in" means.
- Does the interpretation "act" for you, the dreamer?

Once the dream has been interpreted, do recurring dreams stop? In the following days, weeks, and months, does life begin to change? When the interpretation acts for the dreamer, that is what happens.

Is the interpretation confirmed (or not confirmed) by subsequent dreams?

If a dream interpretation is not confirmed, do you have similarly themed dreams with different characters but similar storylines? The dream interpretation is not complete.

Do the events anticipated by the interpretation occur in the dreamer's waking life?

Does your behavior start to change concerning your waking life? When you have correctly interpreted the dream, life can change more authentically. You may break free from old programming that has hindered your life.

An affirmative answer to any one of these questions serves to verify an interpretation.

Step 4: Create a Ritual For The Dream

Without the ritual, the dream is left in the ether and is not adequately embodied by you. When you bring the ceremony into this everyday reality, you are uniting both sides of the coin that constitute yourself — your waking and dreaming life.

Without the dream ritual, the interpretation is not complete.

How To Create Your Ritual Ceremony

The word ceremony comes from the Latin word "awe," so your ritual ceremony aims to create a sense of awe within you and what you are doing. Your dream ritual will be a symbolic behavior consciously performed. A ritual is an art that ties our two halves together; it helps make us whole.

The most potent rituals are the

Conjunction

ones that are subtle, low-key, positive, affirmative, and supportive.

Look at your dream and the interpretation and ask yourself, how I can honor it? What simple and powerful action can I do to honor the dream?

Examples of Dream Rituals

- After having a dream of your childhood home and street, go for a walk down that street.
- Symbolically burning or releasing a lesson that you need to let go of.
- Playing a sport you dreamed about but no longer play.
- Purchasing or reading a book that you receive from a dream character.
- Buying certain products that you loved in your dream (i.e., wind chimes, incense, or a necklace.)
- If you are angry with somebody in the dream, sometimes that could unintentionally spill into your waking life. You could write a long letter to that part of yourself that needs to grow up.
- Drawing out your dream symbols in a mandala.
- A giving back ritual could be as simple as seeing beautiful flowers in your dream and picking some up and letting them go into the ocean as gratitude.
- A dream character is dying, and you discover a negative or painful personality trait that wants to die. Having a funeral for it will release the energy to the great unknown.

Use Common Sense

- Do not do a ritual that will hurt you or another person.
- Do not do a ritual that will get you into trouble.
- Do not get into destructive confrontations with other people.
- Do not use your dreams as an excuse to act out.

- If you dream about making substantial changes in your life, make sure you make them after long and careful consideration.

Format For Interpretation

Step 1: Make Associations

Break each aspect of the dream down and write the associations that you have to each image; this is a process of amplification.

Symbol 1 — Associations

Symbol 2 — Associations

Symbol 3 — Associations

And so on.

Amplify — You must turn up the volume, uncover and unpack the emotional energy within each dream symbol.

Step 2: Inner Connections

Dramatic Structure Of Dream

Setting — Where does the dream take place?

Structure — How is the story of the dream organized?

Exposition — What is the background information of this story?

Protagonists — Who are the main characters of the dream?

Antagonists — Who is active opposition in the dream?

Plot Development: What is the initial situation that propels the dream forward?

The Culmination of The Dream — What is the climax of the dream?

Lysis — What is the result?

Amplify — Personal amplifications to the dream symbols and story structure.

The Dream as a whole

What is your overall feeling about the dream as a whole?

Interconnecting Themes

How do the themes in the Dream connect with your life?

Coagulation

1 ....

2 ....

3 ....

4 ....

Conscious Situation

What is the current conscious situation currently going on in your life?

Dream Series

Are there previous dreams that relate to this dream?

Step 3: The Interpretation

The Dream As a Psychic Fact

How is the dream a factual representation of your life as it is right now?

The Dream Doesn't Tell You What To Do; It Tells You What Is Going On.

How is the dream informing you of your conscious situation in life as it is right now?

Does this dream confirm a previous interpretation?

Answer The Questions:

How does this relate to me and my current life situation?

What conscious attitude does this dream conceal or offset?

What does this concretely mean for me?

Verify The Interpretation:

Does the interpretation "click in" with you?

Does the interpretation "act" for you, the dreamer?

Is the interpretation confirmed (or not confirmed) by subsequent dreams?

Do the events anticipated by the interpretation occur in the dreamer's waking life?

Step 4: Create a Ritual

Your honoring ritual must create a sense of awe and reverence for the teachings you have received. Rituals often mark change and transformation; how will this ritual embody that?

What simple, low-key, positive, affirmative, and supportive symbolic action can you take to honor this dream and its teaching?

Be creative.

Interpreting The Dream

The Dream

I am fishing in an indoor swimming pool in a community center. I am fishing with two friends from my childhood. I keep casting my fishing line out into the water, and I float in an inner tube. I end up catching something, and when I reel it in, it is a large, black gummy bear. I get an acknowledgment from them that I have caught something and that it weighs over 10 pounds. I throw it back in the pool and wonder why I am even fishing in a community swimming pool when we should be fishing in a lake.

Step 1: Amplify Each Dream Symbol

Associations

Friend 1: Childhood friend, got me into trouble, heard him talking negatively about me, has problems with the law.

Friend 2: Childhood friend, famously lazy, funny with a dark sense of humor, doesn't care for himself.

Community swimming pool: Swimming lessons, swimming lengths, boring places, places of pain, and fitness. Something my mother made me do. A sterile place for fishing. Water can represent the subconscious.

I am casting a fishing line: Searching for something, an act of throwing, hoping to attract fish.

Fishing: My father, brother, and grandfather. Something I didn't like as a child, had no patience for, wasn't good at it, Trent River fishing trip with my brother, father, and grandfather.

Fishing in a swimming pool: Looking for fish in a sterile environment, hoping to obtain a goal in the wrong place.

Gummy bear: Something my grandmother used to give me all the time as a kid by the bagful. In her house full of smoke. Something I looked forward to, something I loved to receive, something that communicated she loved me.

Colour black: Powerful and robust color, usually has darker connotations and associations, Baphomet, lack of life, and the shadow.

Distillation

Ten pounds: Lightweight dumbbell at the gym, has weight but still very light.

Acknowledgment from friends: Superficial, wrong kind of reward.

Freshwater lake: Source of life, oxygen, nature, a purer reflection of the psyche.

Step 2: Inner Connections

Dramatic Structure Of Dream

Setting - The dream takes place in a community swimming center, which would be on the turf of my mother; however, the act of fishing would be my father's turf.

Structure - I am in a swimming pool for a fishing competition with friends I know are not a good influence.

Exposition - If I were to use the movie method (on page 81), I would say that I had been spending time with them, and even though I knew it was a stupid idea, I went along with it because I didn't want to be isolated.

Protagonists - I am the leading character, with my friends as background characters.

Antagonists - My friends don't seem to be in direct opposition, however, I am going against my better judgement going along with them.

Plot development - The initial situation is wading in a pool while fishing.

The dream culmination - I catch a large, black gummy bear, and my friends congratulate me.

Lysis - I realize this whole thing is all a farce and wonder why I followed them to fish in a swimming pool instead of a freshwater lake.

Interconnecting Themes

The dream connects with my sometimes over-willingness to do things I know won't be good for me just to hang out with friends, or when I tend to go against my better judgment and do not listen to myself.

While working a job that is not right for me, I have been thinking about how time is critical and how I need to spend more time building skill sets that are authentic to me.

I tend to go behind my own back and thwart my progress; this is more of a shadow dream (more about the shadow on page 48).

Conscious Situation

I moved to a new city and worked a physical labor job that I am not skilled in or desire to be competent in—not making a lot of money, waiting to leave.

Dream Series

It does not connect to any dream series, but the two friends show up in a previous dream together.

Step 3: The Interpretation

The Dream as Psychic Fact

I often do things that don't make sense or do not align with my core principles. I accommodate others' feelings over my own and try to accomplish goals that make sense for others but no sense for me.

The Dream Doesn't Tell You What To Do; It Tells You What Is Going On.

The above answer is pretty straightforward: I am not currently on my life path but am now becoming aware that I need to fish in a place where there is life, authenticity, nature, etc.

Does the dream confirm a previous interpretation?

There is no previous interpretation to confirm.

Answer The Questions

How does this relate to me and my current life situation?

I need to stop fishing (working) in places that are sterile for my soul. It says that I will get rewards no matter what I do, but they will be the wrong kind and not of substantial weight. These rewards — the ones I don't want — will win people's respect that is not necessarily good for me. I have to stop going along with things that I know do not resonate with me and find my life-giving places to "fish" to catch the real fish that I need, instead of prizes in sterile waters.

What conscious attitude does this dream conceal or offset?
The conscious attitude that it conceals is that I often don't think about what I am doing and let unconscious processes or old programming bring me to places that no longer work. I often find myself wasting precious time trying to accomplish a task or adopting a group behavior that does not resonate with my dreaming power. To keep doing this is not to go my own way, and at the end of my life, if I continue to do this, I will realize it will not be my life but a life driven by other people.

What does this concretely mean for me?
It means that I need to start identifying what is uniquely my way and to place greater value on how I spend my time. Otherwise, I will give up control to other people, archetypal energies, and ancestral mythology. I have to keep a closer eye on how I am living out shadow material, ancestral mythology, and how I put others' needs before my own. I need to stop seeking false respect from others instead of following my intuition and fishing in the psyche's life-giving waters. The dying words of my uncle still hold: "Every man must go his own way."

Verify The Interpretation

Does the interpretation "click in" with you?
Yes. Absolutely.

Does the interpretation "act" for you, the dreamer?
We will see.

Is the interpretation confirmed or not confirmed by subsequent dreams?
We will see.

Step 4: The Ritual

For this particular dream, I have bought a bracelet made of paracord and a fishhook to wear. Since the lesson is quite an important one — to continually ask myself If I am fishing in swimming pools or lakes — I need to have this lesson on me at all times.

Increase Your Dream Recall

Make a decision that dreamwork is essential, and you want to start learning from your dreams.

Talk to others about dreams. The more you begin to talk and think about dreams, the likelier you will have them.

Decide the method in which you will record your dreams. The best way is to have a dream journal. Keep your dreaming tools close by so you can record your dreams immediately.

Before you go to bed, remind yourself to remember your dreams in the morning.

When you wake up, don't open your eyes right away; remember the dream before opening your eyes and play it backward in your memory.

Don't look at your phone or electronic devices when you first wake up. They will erase a lot of the dream memory.

Take more B6 vitamins. (University of Adelaide test shows Vitamin B6 increase dream recall)

If you know other people who are into dreaming, join a dream circle. Using social reinforcement can help you remember and record your dreams.

Most importantly, don't be discouraged that you can't remember your dreams. The psyche is like an alchemical furnace, and sometimes it acts more like a pressure cooker. You haven't been dreaming because something is in the pressure cooker. Give it time.

The Transformation of Mercurius

The Archetypes

"Not for a moment dare we succumb to the illusion that an archetype can be finally explained and disposed of...The most we can do is to dream the myth onwards and give it a modern dress."
– From The Archetypes of the Collective Unconscious, Paragraph 271, The Collected Works of C.G. Jung

What are archetypes, and why are they important?

Archetypes are energies, aspects, and patterns of your psychology that are mostly unconscious. They are mysterious and primarily instinctual. They are the culmination of our 2-million-year-old collective unconscious. They appear in dreams to be understood and worked through by you, the dreamer, in order to progress in your individuation process. They are essential to recognize and work with because they are like energetic doorways and teachers. Archetypes will help you understand why you act the way you act, how you think the way you think, and once they are worked with and understood, they will help you transform your life and become united with the Self.

Archetypes are powerful transpersonal energies occurring within you at this very moment. Sometimes they jockey to take you over in your entirety. They are compelling aspects of psychic energy and to be respected. They morph and grow over time, depending on the amount of personal work and maturation you have done.

The definition of an archetype, according to Carl Jung, is:

An archetype is a universal and archaic pattern that comes from the collective unconscious. They are mysterious and are often hidden once they enter into the unconscious, they primarily influence your instinctual drive. They are highly developed elements of your unconscious and expressed differently through each culture. They are often expressed and discovered through stories, art, myth, religions or dreams.

Plato's Allegory of The Cave

The Dream Ego

The Role You Play, and The Way You Act In Dreams

The Dream Ego is the role you are playing as a witness or actor in the dream and represents your felt sense of identity as it is right now. How you think, act and feel within the dream, relates to how you think, act and feel in daily life. The dream ego will act exactly as you tend to do while awake in the world.

The Self is the architect of your dream world, and the role you play as the Dream Ego is an integral part of the dream. How you behave in the dream, is how the Self will see you as you are right now. You will not always interact with or see each of the Archetypes in your dream, but it is a guarantee that you will experience the Dream Ego in each dream because that is you either witnessing or acting in the dream.

Everything that you see in the dream is an attempt made by the Self to guide you back to your own authentic center. The dream will act as a mirror to the Dream Ego spurring it to bring out your shortcomings, potentials, tendencies, and unhealthy behaviours that may not be fully known to you right now. You can reflect on the actions of your Dream Ego to see how this relates to your behaviour in daily life, and if this is helping or hindering your personal growth. How your Dream Ego interacts with the dream images, characters or symbols is a lesson, it can be a source of encouragement or a warning.

The Dream Ego In Dreams

The Dream Ego is you as the role you play within the dream. It can be as yourself, a child, a witness, a scuba diver, a princess, anything where you see the dream through your own eyes as actor or witness. It is you as the experiencer, and you don't need to be exactly as you. The Dream Maker has lessons to teach you on your way to personal growth, and if you are experiencing the dream as a different character other than as yourself. This may be how you are acting in day to day life.

Working with the Dream Ego

If you dream that you are a princess, how does that relate to how you see yourself consciously or unconsciously? Are you being given a task that you are not sure that you can do, but a positive dream figure is assuring you that you can? Maybe listen to the advice that is being given to you. What actions, thoughts or moods do you experience in the dream? Is this helping you or hindering you in your life? Are your actions contrary to how you think you are as a person? For example, do you believe yourself to be a thoughtful and caring person, but in the time of need of a dream character you give superficially instead of actually helping? Remember the dream meaning is not congratulatory, it is giving you hard pills to swallow that is medicine for your personal growth, and progress of your soul.

You can use associations with the actions you are taking within the dream

- The Dream Ego is fighting a main power character
- The Dream Ego wakes up from the dream

From the list above, add a statement that comes in as an unconscious belief that is associated with that action.

- The Dream Ego is fighting a main power character (hurt others, before they hurt you)
- The Dream Ego wakes up from the dream (it is easier to escape than to deal with my challenges)

Dream Ego Questions

What is the Dream Ego's journey through the dream, and what is it going through?

What kind of characteristics do you notice about the Dream Ego?

What are the attitudes and emotions behind the Dream Ego's actions? How does this relate to how you act in your daily life?

What are the issues that you (the Dream Ego) are dealing with in the dream?

If you dream that you are different than how you present in waking reality. Using association, how does this dream character relate to how you feel or perceive yourself at an unconscious level?

How does your behaviour as the dream ego fit into the wholeness of the dream?

How is the dream ego led through the dream to the lysis? What is the lesson the dream ego needs to learn?

The Persona

Your Social Mask

The Persona is the most surface level of all your archetypes. It is the mask you wear to fulfill specific roles in society, like being a doctor, a parent, a gang member, a CEO, a spouse, a victim, etc. Whatever part you are currently playing in society,

Greek Drama Masks

you compromise with the Self to create a performance of the characters you can identify with.

It is normal, however, to have a Persona but it is not healthy to identify with it. In other cases, some people like to identify strongly with the Persona of a public figure. They attempt to wear that person's mask and hope to have it as their own. Once somebody does this, they stop growing, and it will cause problems when they face difficulties later in life. You stop growing and evolving as a person when you start to identify with and try to become the Persona of someone else.

The Persona in Dreams

The easiest way to identify the Persona is by dreaming and noticing the clothes that appear in your dreams — whether they be uniforms, costumes, clothes you might typically wear or not, as well as nakedness. The Persona will usually appear in clothes symbolic of the position and role you are playing now and can also signify what you are about to become or need to evolve into.

Working with The Persona

Identifying your Persona in your dreams will help make the roles you are playing in the waking world more conscious, and you can stop and reflect if this is the role you genuinely want to be playing.

Ask yourself:

What kind of person wears these clothes?

Are you with a group of people wearing a costume?

Are you putting on any masks in a dream? If so, what kind?

Are there clothes you want to wear in a dream? If so, what kind?

The Persona can sometimes be an overlooked aspect of the dream interpretation, and it is as essential in dream interpretation as the other archetypes. Identifying our Persona can help you shed light on the unconscious roles you are playing in life, and by understanding it, you can decide for yourself if you want to keep playing it or not.

The Shadow

The Thing, A Person, Has No Wish To Be

"Find out what a person fears most, and that is where they will develop next"
— C.G Jung (From Owning Your Shadow)

The shadow is where we find our purpose, our great work, our higher calling in life. By doing the shadow work, we reveal the great light within. It is not an easy road, but it is the way.

According to Jung, the shadow is: "that hidden, repressed, for the most part, an inferior and guilt-laden personality whose ultimate ramifications reach back into our animal ancestors' realm ... If it has been believed hitherto that the human Shadow was the source of evil, it can now be ascertained on closer investigation that the unconscious man, that is his Shadow does not consist only of morally reprehensible tendencies, but also displays a number of good qualities, such as normal instincts, appropriate reactions, realistic insights, creative impulses, etc."

Nigredo Stage

The Germans had a word for it. They called it the "Hintergedanke," which is the ulterior motive or hidden agenda of your actions. The deep, deep part of yourself that drives your actions is your shadow. We all have a shadow — every one of us.

One of the best ways to identify your shadow in waking reality is to watch your visceral emotional reactions to other people's behaviors. We get angry about what we think is a negative trait in another, but, in actuality, we are reacting to the repressed aspects in ourselves. The qualities in others you do not like are a part of you, and you can recognize them as part of your shadow.

You know you are being possessed by the shadow when you are "acting out" or exhibiting little control over your behavior.

It is often shadow material that is the root problem between friends and partners.

The shadow can also be the energy we need in life, our source of vitality. By integrating your shadow and becoming more aware of it, you can use it and even find a good use for that energy. The shadow can possess the most creative and valuable aspects of your character.

> *"Generally, one makes friends with one's shadow figure. Tell me who your friends are, and I have the whole panorama of your good and bad qualities."*
> — Marie-Louise Von Franz:
> The Way Of The Dream.

The Shadow In Dreams

The shadow will appear in dreams as somebody of the same sex as you. Sometimes, you will know them. Sometimes, it will appear frightening, like a zombie, a dark shape, a scary figure, or an unseen thing. It is someone or something we feel uneasy about, like something sinister or threatening. It can appear as an aggressive or threatening animal. Or, on the contrary, it can appear as a friendly and helpful person in an otherwise nasty person. It can also be a character with darker characteristics or skin than the dreamer.

If you encounter these energies in your dreams, it is essential to use the associative method described in Step 1 of the dream interpretation process (page 21). Gossip about the shadow figure, who they are, what they represent, and what they want with you? How can they become your ally?

Usually, dreams of being chased are your shadow trying to catch up to you. It wants to be recognized and accepted by you.

It is only what we fear and reject that overpowers us. Learning to face your shadow could lead you to profound changes, transformation, and growth in your life.

The shadow stands in the way of full Anima/Animus access (which we will learn about starting on page 52). It is the nest where your Anima/Animus lives. You must integrate it consciously before the more profound work with Anima/Animus can begin, or at least before it can be successful. Your shadow is the dark knight that stands at the gate of the castle and challenges you to a fight before you can get in.

Keep an eye out for shadow figures in your dreams to understand what your shadow is and find ways to use it as an ally instead of an enemy.

Owning Your Shadow

Throughout our culture, the story of good vs. evil echoes across time. Your shadow work is about the integration of both because you are both. Like galaxies in space, both aspects of yourself gradually come within one another's orbit and eventually collide. Owning your shadow is when both galaxies collide. The two must become one.

Unity with your Shadow is your goal.

Take a look at who you are now:

Are you timid? Your shadow is ferocious.

Are you an upstanding citizen? Your shadow is a delinquent.

Are you known as a tough guy? Your shadow is a softie.

Are you a free spirit? Your shadow is a homebody.

The shadow works as an equal and opposite to your Persona. Owning your shadow starts with identifying your shadow in your dreams, through dream characters and frightening entities. Identify them, who they are, and start to actively incorporate your shadow into your life, healthily and positively.

Are you timid in waking reality? If you are dreaming of fighting, join a boxing class.

Are you known as an enforcer in waking reality? If you are dreaming of poets, maybe it's time to start writing.

Even though these are examples, let the Dream Maker take the lead. Once you recognize your shadow, ask yourself: How can you allow your shadow to express itself healthily? Otherwise, it will continue to go behind your own back and thwart your progress.

The Contra-Sexual Archetype

The most revised and controversial topic of Carl Jung's Dream Analysis and Psychological theory is the Anima & Animus (unconscious feminine and masculine) in a person's psyche. It is so controversial because it focuses on gender issues and the differences of masculine and feminine psychology. However, the Contra-sexual archetype lies beyond the influence of society, culture, family, and friends. It is a relating function that helps you mate and relate to the opposite sex and helps you reach your fulfillment. It dwells in the deep and impersonal house of your unconscious beyond the scope of your conscious awareness. It acts as a psychopomp, meaning it introduces your conscious personality (dream ego) to your deeper inner world. It will reveal to you the deeper undeveloped attitudes, feelings, stirrings, and thoughts hidden in the deeper and darker recesses of your mind. The Anima/us is an essential life form that shapes your individuality and has influenced cultures and societies worldwide. The Anima/us is beyond the range of your perception, and you can only understand it by how it reveals itself to you in your dreams and how you project it onto members of the opposite sex.

Mercury And Sulfur Personified

Your Anima/us will usually appear in your dream as either a character or group of the opposite sex that you do not know or as a masculine or feminine symbol/animal/mythological figure. It will introduce you to the deeper aspects of your personality and unconscious. In addition to revealing your inner psychic storehouse, your relationship to your Contra-sexual will be projected onto members of the opposite sex for a romantic partner if you are heterosexual. If you are homosexual, the inner Contra-sexual often appears as a helpful sibling.

In a sense, the Contra-sexual could be considered "Maya," the creator of the grand illusions; under the unconscious influence of the Anima/us, your Ego will live in the world primarily based on endless projections. We can be truly amazed by how persistent and distorted these projections/illusions can be; even when there are severe flaws in our world view, we can still unwaveringly believe in them.

The Contra-sexual Archetype of the Anima/us is an undeveloped function of our unconscious. The more masculine a man's outer attitude appears to be, the more feminine feelings appear in his unconscious and vice versa.

The next section will help you identify the contra-sexual archetype in your dreams and how you can learn from it.

The Anima

The Feminine Side To a Man, And How He Relates To Women

The shadow has to deal with your Ego's hidden aspects; the Anima brings you into and reveals your unconscious's hidden characteristics.

You are a Man, and also a Woman. There is a Contra-sexual aspect of your unconscious within you, known as the Anima or your feminine side. It exists as something absolutely other, which is true for all men, old, young, gay, straight, married, or single. Every man has one in their psyche without exception, and it is present right from birth.

Rebis: Royal Hermaphrodite With The Tree of The Moon

By not doing dreamwork, and keeping your Anima unconscious, everything the Anima is, will be projected. Later in life, if you do not develop a conscious relationship with your Anima, life will lose its vividness, its vitality, and in some extreme cases, its meaning. The Anima is not a specific inner woman, but it is an internal Contra-sexual energy that manifests within the psyche. It is an inner relating function that will allow you to complete yourself in other ways other than just mating and relating to the opposite sex. It helps you complete yourself fully, whatever it may be out in the world.

> *"When the Anima is pregnant within the dream, what is going to be born is individuality."*
> — Murray Stein:
> Jungs Concept of the Anima

A few important things to note about your Anima

- Your Fathers Anima will influence your (his son's) Anima.
- Not every woman in your dreams will be your Anima.
- Your Anima is much further away from you and more mysterious than your shadow; it will begin to reveal more profound aspects of yourself when it starts to appear.
- Your Anima will present itself as an inner figure that you are attracted to, that you are drawn to.

How to spot your Anima in your dreams:

The Anima does not just appear as a female, but also as female symbols.

Be on the lookout in your dreams for:

- A beautiful feminine image or essence that you are drawn too
- Fairies
- Influential Feminine Figures
- Women you don't know
- Ballet Dancers
- Nurses
- Prostitutes
- Teachers

- Queen
- Hairdresser

Feminine types of animals like a:
- Cow
- Cat
- Tiger
- Butterfly
- Doe
- Swan
- Lioness

Or objects like:
- A Cave
- Or a Ship.

The Anima is anything that can be related to feminine figures. An influential Anima figure can also be a damsel in distress, which would mean a symbol that a man's Anima is in danger or is dying, and only a kiss or breath of life can resurrect it so that the man can transform his life.

How The Anima Functions in a Man's Psyche

Anima Functioning Poorly

Men who are being overwhelmed by their Anima tend to withdraw into their inner world's hurt feelings and be frequently moody. A man's Anima will release overwhelming emotions like gas into his ego awareness. His relationships tend to be filled with conflict because his feelings are too powerful for him to control. The man's Ego will become identified with his Anima, which, as a rule, is bogged down with emotions and hypersensitive. When a man's Anima is not highly developed, he will not be able to cope with overwhelming moods and instead will be drawn in much deeper.

Properly Functioning Anima

When a Man's Anima is functioning properly, he will have access to tenderness, empathy, a feeling of an inner helper and being supported, he will not tend to dwell on hurt feelings, he will be heart-led, have a relationship to life, have authentic relationships with women, have a greater connection to life, and a more profound sense of fulfillment.

To understand the Anima, you must Wed The Anima.

"He must come to terms with his personal Anima, the femininity that belongs to him, that accompanies and supplements him but may not be allowed to rule him."
— *Emma Jung, Anima, and Animus.*

All fetuses begin in the womb as female. If there is no Y chromosome present, then the fetus will continue to develop as a female. A man, initially, starts his life out as a woman. By learning to identify your Anima in your dreams, you will begin to understand how you relate to women and life. You can understand how these projections are helping or hindering your life, and once you identify the illusion, you can break free from the projections that are holding you back. The Anima is the bridge to the unconscious, the psychopomp, the doorway to the deeper.

You, as a man, if you wish to take the ultimate journey inward, and complete your mission of wholeness, will need to identify, accept, and make partners with your Anima.

First you must take stock of the interactions you have with unknown women and feminine symbols in your dreams:

- Are they helpful or hindering?
- How are these common themes being projected onto the women in your day to day life and relationships?
- Can you see a correlation between the relationships with females in your life and the dreams you are having surrounding your Anima figures?
- How do the situations in your dreams relate to how you feel about yourself and life at a deeper level?
- How do you feel your relationship is with your Anima? How does your Anima show up in your life and your relationships with other people?

Learning to identify how your Anima is present in your life and working with it will require some help. If you are serious about your development, it should be performed with a trained Jungian Psychoanalyst.

The Animus

The Masculine Side to a Female, and How She Relates To Men.

The shadow has to deal with your Ego's hidden aspects; the Animus brings you into the hidden and deeper aspects of your unconscious.

You are a woman, and also a man. Within you, there is a Contra-sexual aspect of your unconscious, which is known as the Animus or your masculine side. It exists as something absolutely other, which is true for all women, old, young, gay, straight, married, or single. Every woman has one in their psyche without exception. Your Animus will reveal himself in your dreams, and the situations you are involved in with your Animus in the dream will project itself onto the relationships you have with men. It is an inner relating function that will allow you to complete yourself in other ways other than just mating and relating to the opposite sex. It helps you complete yourself fully, whatever it may be out in the world.

Rebis: Alchemy Hermaphroditus

A few important things to note about your Animus:

- Your Mother's Animus will influence your (her daughters) Animus.

- Not every man in your dreams will be your Animus.
- Your Animus is much further away from you and more mysterious than your shadow; he will begin to reveal more profound aspects of yourself when he starts to appear.
- Your Animus will present himself as an inner figure that you are attracted to, that you are drawn to.
- Your inner masculine is an internal unconscious drive that reveals itself to you through your dreams.

The Animus Revealed in Dreams

Learning to spot your Animus in your dreams will help you understand what kind of relationship and personality traits belong to your inner masculine. By keeping a note about your dreams and the situations you have with your Animus, you will discover how you project your inner masculine onto your relationships with men and how your relationship with your Animus is helping or hindering your life.

Animus Dream Characters & Symbols

- Men you don't know in your waking life.
- A Perfect mate
- A Magician
- A King
- Dwarves
- A Mythical Creature
- A Quick Change Artist
- Artist
- Aviator
- Mechanic

A group of men, such as:
- A Council
- A Court

- A Gathering of Wise Men
- Soldiers
- Sailors

Masculine Animals such as:
- Eagle
- Bull
- Lion

The Animus is anything that can be related to male figures. An influential Animus figure can also be a drunkard, a harmful and destructive image of a woman's Animus that is in danger of harboring self-destructive personality traits.

Animus Functions In a Woman's Psyche

Animus Functioning Poorly

Women who are experiencing an Animus Problem, they are usually overcome with emotionally charged thoughts and opinions which she can feel controlled by, instead of in control of. She can wreak havoc on her relationships with a tendency to bring the energy of a bully and exude aggressive behavior. People around her will start to build protective bubbles around themselves when they are with her. Even though she may want to be receptive and intimate, it is tough for her to do so because her Ego is at the whims of these disruptive and invasive emotional energies. The Animus is a powerful personality that is not aligned with the Ego. It is the other. Her relationships with men will usually be unhealthy ones.

Animus Functioning Positively

Women who have a good relationship with their Animus have a strong sense of internal strength in her center; she will display a useful capability for logical and rational thought and have an inner bridge to knowledge and creative thinking.

Working With Your Animus

First, you must take stock of the interactions you have with unknown men or male figures in your dreams:

- Are they helpful or hindering?
- How are these common themes being projected onto the men in your day-to-day life and relationships?
- Can you see a correlation between the relationships with males in your life and the dreams you are having surrounding your animus figures?
- How do the situations in your dreams relate to how you feel about yourself at a deeper level?
- How do you feel your relationship is with your Animus? How does your Animus show up in your life and your relationships with other people?

Learning to identify how your Animus is present in your life and working with it will require some help. If you are serious about your development, it should be performed with a trained Jungian Psychoanalyst.

The Self

Realizing The God Within

At the center of your psychic landscape sits the Self. It is the prime archetype, the "ONE" archetype from which all others derive from. It is the magnetic center of your psychic universe that guides your Ego to its true north. The Self is the transcendent function of your psyche which produces symbols of wholeness within the dream; they often occur as squares or circles. We call these square or circle images of the Self a 'Mandala.'

Phoenix Rising From The Ashes

When the Self begins to get involved with the individuation process, the other archetypes will appear, like the Shadow, the Animus/Anima, and the soul image. Once it has begun, this process will start to reveal a path that leads the way to self-realization or "The God Within." Where the Anima/us is the mediating function of the unconscious to the conscious, the Self will appear as the Wise Old Man/ Woman, which is like the representative speaker of the 2-million-year-old collective unconscious.

The Ego will be unable to carry out the momentous task of individuation by itself, and it will need the help of an angel type of being to assist. When your Ego is connected to the transcendent center of the Self, it is beyond the narcissistic short-sighted goals of the Ego for short term gains. Instead, you would have an ego-free quality because you would be consulting a much deeper source of your unconscious.

The Self is the complete merging process between the conscious and unconscious in a person. It is the wholeness of yourself. By far, the Self is the most complex and transpersonal of all the archetypes. It is associated with the deepest levels of your psyche and is extremely powerful. It is the end goal of Carl Jung's individuation process. It is God within us.

The Self In Dreams

The Self can be identified in dream imagery by the following symbols.

Mandalas: A flower, gold coins, a ball, a globe, a round target to shoot at, a clock (circular movement), a circular fountain, a roundabout circle for cars, a town square, a round table, a spiral

People: An aged seer or priestess, a wise old man or woman, a young child (i.e., the end or the beginning), the Cosmic Man, hermaphrodite, Royal Couple, an inner voice, guardian spirit, daemon, or genius.

Mythical animals: Phoenix (bird consumed in flames and reborn from its ashes), Ouroboros (snake biting its tail), totem spirits. A snake is often also a symbol of the Self that represents the extreme opposites within the Self.

Things: Items that serve as the guide or goal of a quest, like the Holy Grail, the Elixir of Immortality, the Star of Bethlehem, the Philosopher's Stone, or a hidden treasure.

The Self can manifest as a wisdom figure, a talking plant, a water pool — something transpersonal and on the fringes of mythical and magical.

Understanding the messages of the Self.

When working with the Self's images, it is crucial to realize the type of dynamite energy it brings. This is not an easy archetype; it has an intense solar nature, it is not easy to understand or easy to work with, and the Self's images are quite rare.

At this stage of your dream work, it would be highly imperative to be working with somebody. It is said that nobody transforms alone, and to be appropriately transformed; you need helpers, especially at this stage. You can find helpers in the forms or therapists, shamans, myths, rituals, rites of passage, ceremonies, or transformational workshops. Remember, it is always important to do your due diligence on who you are working with.

Not all work on the Self is pure light; heavy energy is attached to integrating the Self. Since the Self is the most significant power of all in the psyche, it can cause a person to disconnect from reality, indulge in megalomania, and believe that the person has solved and understood all cosmic riddles. Such a person may lose touch with their very humanness, which is the most precious thing we have in this life. If this happens, then the individuation process has not been completed.

The Self is hard to interpret and integrate because the psychic energies that accompany it are like strong solar waves. Not even the most skilled shamans can fully integrate it. They can only develop the skill to fly closer to the sun without getting burned.

Working alone with these archetypes can be challenging. It is best to work with a skilled analyst to gain a fundamental understanding of them.

Identifying The Messages Of The Self

How does the Self like to show up? Are there any patterns?

What type of messages is it conveying to you?

How is the Self guiding your life?

The Fountain of Life

Types Of Dreams

Big Dreams

Prophetic, Life-Changing, Vivid, Unforgettable

Big Dreams are the dreams that you remember for your entire life, and they are considered the most precious jewels in the psychic treasure house. The reason that they are much different than ordinary dreams is that they are full of rich symbolism that is beyond the scope of everyday life. They seem to draw from the collective unconscious's deepest level and have a poetic and beautiful force about them. Big dreams usually show up in critical phases of life, which are early youth, puberty, the onset of middle age (36-40), the beginning of old age, and within sight of death.

These dreams are quite hard to interpret because they transcend personal associations. These dreams possess mythological motifs, archetypal products, and they are not concerned with personal experience, but more so, general ideas.

Little Dreams

Day-To-Day Dreams

Little dreams are mundane and forgettable content. They are not as emotionally charged as Big Dreams, although essential and important to work through. They do not carry the psychic punch that the Big Dreams have. Most dreams you have will be little dreams.

Dream Series

Dream series is a running story or series that provides us with the information we need to understand and develop through our life as it is right now. Dreams respond to our changing attitudes of consciousness and act as a rudder to get us back on course toward individuation.

When you keep a dream journal, you can see how some dreams set up other dreams. Sometimes, even one dream acts as a seed that gives birth to a dream nine months later.

Dream series are not so black and white, and as usual, it will all depend on the dreamer. If the dreamer does not remember many dreams, the ones that they remember will ultimately be the dream series.

Sometimes, the dream series will be all the dreams that are happening through a transformation or significant emotional change in your life, like a move, a career change, a divorce, or a family member's death. Watching those dreams can be a dream series. The total of the dreams during a transitionary period is a dream series. It is not a definite number of dreams; it could be 10, 20, or 100. Working with ten dreams at a time is a way to keep up to date on your psychic situation.

Death and Destruction

Visions of Transformation

When you dream of death, it is rarely a prophetic dream. Since death and transformation are the same things to the psyche, it means just that, transformation.

When working on a death dream, it is essential to look at previous dreams to understand the current dream better. Look at your life and see what is changing or what needs to change. Remember: the interpretation is the one we most likely do not want to hear. If you dream of a loved one dying, how is that relationship changing?

Homoerotic

Reconnecting with Disconnected Aspects Of Yourself

Homoerotic dreams, or dreams of having a sexual experience with the same sex, are an expression by the Dream Maker to complete the character of the dreamer's gender. When fully integrated, it would make the dreamer a fuller version of their masculinity or femininity. It helps your True Self integrate who and what you are meant to be while on the path of individuation. Suppose you have a sexual encounter with a person of the same sex as you. What kind of person are they? What are their character traits?

Repetitive Dreams

Important Message

The Dream Maker will repeat dreams and messages until they are finally understood, accepted, and worked through in waking life. These deserve special attention because the message is an important one.

Nightmares

Very Important Messages

Nightmares are dreams that will frighten the dreamer. The Dream Maker has a tendency to overdramatize, nightmares are crucial messages from the Guiding Self and need extra special attention. They will either point to urgent problems or new problems on the horizon. They may also expose outgrown obstacles or invite the dreamer to be aware of opportunities to grow and heal that the dreamer once was afraid to risk. Nightmares tend to support the death of currently held attitudes and the dreamer's ego outlook, so they will sometimes include death and dismemberment.

Numbers in Dreams

Symbols Of The Self

When numbers are seen in dreams they have a much deeper meaning than just a random occurrence. They are more archetypal than common dream symbols and are symbols of the self, that are coming through to your consciousness awareness. Numbers in dreams link us to something larger than ourselves, the like universe, the divine, or a cosmic reality. When they appear in your dream, they should be treated with the same respect as an archetype. Numbers come to give you advice, to show you a path, ad give you a message that you need to work with.

Use free association when working with numbers to see what comes up and what they mean to you. Play with the numbers; how do you think the Dream Maker is presenting them to you? Roll with whatever comes up. Add them up, break them down, discover ancient meanings. Dig deep until you find that "aha" moment.

Do they add up to something?

Do they bring up an association?

Colors In Dreams

The Mother Tongue of the Unconscious

Color connects to our emotions. Consider the expressions: green with envy, feeling blue, or I was so mad. I saw red. Color is symbolic of a psychic process, and using your associations with the colors in your dream can add tremendous depth to the interpretation of your dreams.

Suppose there is a significant color in your dream, like a blue room, an orange object, or a red gift. Make sure to pay close attention to it because the unconscious is trying to get this point across to you.

Highly Emotional Characters

If somebody is angry or sad, or you find yourself interacting with a character like a homeless person or a clown, ask yourself: how does this highly emotional or strange person relate to you and your life? You can ask questions like what part of you is angry, and how can you relate to this angry person? What part of you feels homeless? Remember that the dream is where you are all the characters. It reveals aspects of your consciousness that you do not wish to disclose to others.

Children

Meeting the Inner Child

> *"And a little child shall lead them."*
> *– Isaiah 11:6*

If the Dream Maker shows you children, babies, or even a pregnant woman, it is usually referring to your inner child. It shows you the child level of your unconscious in order to see everything unfinished with your process of growth, your relationships to people, attitudes, and productive skills. It is the child in you that hasn't become an adult yet.

The children will hint at the potentials and possibilities lying dormant in the psyche, and ways to renew your spirit will come to light.

Animals

Lead Us to the Kingdom

When you encounter an animal in your dream, it has much to do with your instinctual drive, the associations you place on the animal and even mythological motifs associated with that animal.

When you work with animals, it is crucial to know about the mythological amplification and include them in your interpretation. You can also use the movie theatre exercise on page 81 to create a play in your mind's eye and decide which roles the animals play in your dream image.

Remember, the personal associations and motifs will have to be woven into the interpretation.

As in all fairy tales, folk legends, and myths, it is meaningful to note that across all cultures, interactions with animals are always held in high regard and are not to be dismissed as trivial. Sometimes they are trusted, sought out or avoided, protected, or killed. However, meeting an animal in a dream, in one way or another, is significant, and you should pay attention to this interaction.

Mythological Motifs

Legends in Disguise

Mythological dreams will often disguise themselves and will not always appear in their usual costumes, as in the stories you learned in school or through movies and books. They will usually emerge in small bursts.

We can correctly assume that the dream has taken on mythic psychic energy when shapeshifting occurs, like when one thing turns into another or when objects or animals can speak and behave like human beings.

Sometimes they can be masked in everyday occurrences like the hunt for a cup (Quest for the Holy Grail), for example, or apprenticing for a master electrician (Zeus). Look at the storylines, and once you can identify that the dream has indeed taken on a mythic structure, see if there are similar myths. Get to know the myth and how it applies to your life.

Protector/Persecutor

These are usually trauma based dreams where the dreamer's psyche has not been able to face or process the painful trauma that they have endured. They were once a protector type figure in childhood and it has now turned into a persecutor type figure to shield the dreamer from their trauma later in life. Sometimes they can be a Fairy Godmother in their youth that was their only friend, an angel, or a very helpful figure. The figure could be the same or has morphed into something that is now preventing the dreamer from moving on with their life. They can appear as inner demons, devils, monsters, witches, shadow figures anything that gives you terrible fright. These types of dreams are a familiar fantasy and they are heavy, and dynamite material. These types of dreams can house excruciating pain for the dreamer and it is important to tread very carefully with these dreams. If you are experiencing these types of dreams, please consider speaking with a Jungian Analyst to understand and heal yourself. It will be hard, but very worth it in the end.

The dove rising from the four elements as symbol of the spirit freed from the embrace of Physis.

Dream Amplifications

Strengthening Your Dreamwork Through Exercises

Ten Dreams (To finding the complex)
Worksheet located on page 95.

To discover the hidden personal challenge you are currently facing, consult your last ten dreams. To do this, take your previous ten dreams and find the central conflict in each one. On page 95, there is an example of how to draw a ten dream diagram. Put each conflict into one circle, and the main conflict(s) in the center circle. Find the recurring conflict (there could be 1-3), and there you will discover the underlying and sometimes even hidden challenge/complex in your life right now.

Getting to Know Your Inner Dream Community
Located on page 96.

Get to know the types of characters who show up in your dreams regularly. Are there people, animals, or beings making a regular appearance? They are your inner dreaming community. Your dream parts are your process. Get to know them and the characters who play significant roles. You might find some characters wear different costumes but have similar characteristics.

Try to draw them if you can. Ask yourself why they keep coming around and how they are trying to help you. Within you, all dream characters are trying to teach you a valuable lesson.

Your Inner Animals

Located on page 103

What kind of animal energies are you embodying in your life currently?

Go through all your entries and discover the animals that appear in your dreams. Are there any recurring animals that are consistently surfacing? Are there any that left a strong impression or made an unusual appearance? Make a note of these and put them in your dream journal, and use the exercises on page 103 for guidance. Answer the questions about each animal. What tendencies of this animal are you enacting, need to embody, or need to let go of? What myths are associated with this animal?

The Dream Ego

Located on Page 117

How do you behave in your waking life?

What you, as the observer, do within the dream, the actions you take, and the characters you play will tell you a lot about how you behave in your day-to-day life, whether you are a bystander, fighting, running, swimming, or playing a role like a princess, or a shaman. Do you get anxious, scared, have a fight or flight response, or hide from attackers? All these types of behaviors will give you clues on how you (the Dream Ego) act in the world. Make notes of what you, as the witness, are doing. How does this translate to how you behave in your current life? How do you fall back on these behaviors? Do these types of behaviors help or hinder you in your life?

Your Persona

Located on page 124

Throughout the drama of life, what role and character are you playing?

Your dream entries will reveal clues about your Persona. It will reveal itself as the type of clothes you are wearing in your dream. Clothing will represent the dominant type of person you are playing in the world currently. Make notes of any kind of clothes or costumes you're wearing — or perhaps not wearing — and the circumstances around the dream.

Discover Your Shadow

Located on page 132

Your shadow is the aspect of yourself that you do not wish to be. The part that remains hidden has ulterior motives, can be disrespectful, ungrateful, and is not the person we are trying to portray. However, our shadow is a source of great vitality, and if we learn to embrace it and use it healthily, it will become a great ally to us.

We all have a shadow, you included. Make notes of the characters in your dream who are of the same sex as you and keep reappearing. They will represent your shadow. In the Shadow Work Exercises of Dream Speak, in order of frequency, write out who keeps appearing (whether it's friends and acquaintances, characters from movies or books, celebrities, or characters you don't know at all). Then write out character traits about them, gossip about them, and describe them as if you were explaining them to somebody else. Make note if they are enacting similar things in each dream.

Meeting Your Anima/Animus

Located on page 139

The Anima and Animus dream characters will be much more elusive than your Shadow characters. They visit infrequently and can be hard to spot. You may not even see them much.

In this amplification, note the dream characters of the opposite sex as you and that you do not know. They don't have to be human; they could be a fairy or a dwarf. They could also appear as a human that has a significant part in the dream.

Make a note about who they are as they appear. Include what they are doing, what you would guess that they want with you, and record character details. Play around with it. What is the background story? How did you come to meet them? Get to know these figures, learn from them, work with them, and turn them into an ally. You can recognize Anima/Animus energies in the Anima and Animus sections on page 139.

Lucid Dreaming

Lucid dreaming has been practiced cross-culturally for ages. The ability to achieve lucidity comes easy for some and needs practice for others. Many studies prove that we all can lucid dream, and there are many different ways to achieve this state.

Of all the ways to do it, this is the most effective for me.

Step 1: Set an intention that you want to become lucid while dreaming. Then commit to "reality checking," where you pause during the day and ask yourself, "Is this real? Am I dreaming?" This will bring you back to the present moment and help you scan your current reality and make observations about it. Convince yourself if it is a dream or if it is not.

The more you remind yourself that you want to become lucid with intense emotion, the faster it will happen. You can use dream anchors like stopping and looking at your hands, carrying a talisman in your pocket (like Inception), or stopping at each door you enter to feel it and ask the question, "Is this real? Am I dreaming?" Taking naps with the specific intention of achieving lucidity and tracking your process in a journal is very beneficial to this process.

In Tibetan dream yoga, yogis focus on the letter A (ཨ) glowing in the middle of their chest while they lay down to sleep. Staying conscious of it as they fall asleep helps them cross into dreaming and become lucid.

Step 2: Recognize that you are dreaming. When you are dreaming, it is necessary to recognize what is going on and use one of the dream anchors and questions you have been using to achieve lucidity during your everyday practice.

The dream will give you hints and clues to recognize that you are dreaming. They will include:

- When you can't tell what time it is (looking at a clock and the numbers are jumbled)
- When you question your reality in a dream (why am I back in elementary school?)
- Falling and not hurting yourself
- Drinking, but not drinking water
- Falling in water and not getting wet
- Something else that is out of the ordinary to your everyday experience

When you notice it, immediately use your dream anchor and do a reality check (the best practice is to bring your hands up and look at them and then look around). Ask yourself, "Is this real? Am I dreaming?" A common practice is to poke your hand with your index finger. If it goes through your palm, you are dreaming. Sometimes the excitement of becoming lucid will wake up the dreamer. If this happens, spin around in a circle. It will keep you grounded in the dream.

Step 3: What to do when becoming lucid. The possibilities are quite endless, but you must ask yourself why you want to control your dreams? Lucid dreaming is best for exploration and co-creation. It is like an active imagination on steroids.

Step 4: Dream Journal. It is a rare occurrence to lucid dream on your first try. In your Dream Journal, make a note of any time that you questioned your reality. Underline that moment and write, "should have known I was dreaming." The consistency in recognizing that you are dreaming while journaling helps build the bridge to lucidity.

This four-step process will eventually help you achieve lucidity if you are persistent at it. You can also use dreaming plants like Calea Zacatechichi (described on page 88).

Lucid dreaming has many possible benefits, like obtaining inner knowledge, receiving creative ideas, and conversing with your Shadow or Anima/Animus archetype. It can become dangerous, however, when we try and control the dreaming. Being in the dream and hijacking it will disrupt the messages the unconscious wants to bestow upon you.

Create Something From The Dream

Did you find something beautiful in your dream? A necklace? A poem? A song? A work of art?

Create it in your waking life. Bring the dream over to this reality and make it real. Carry it around with you. It brings a certain amount of transpersonal energy and magic into your life. By bringing more of the images and objects into this side of life, you begin to enmesh both sides of your life (dreaming and waking) together.

If you are stuck, you can also draw a mandala about your dream. Draw a circle, and then within that circle, draw people, images, objects, and colors that come to you. Don't force this and see how it turns out.

Using Dreams To Solve Problems

Before you go to sleep, spend about 30 minutes focusing on the problem you need a solution for. Focus intensely on it, and close your eyes, and imagine that you have put that problem energetically on a sheet of paper, and then write "solved" on that piece of paper and crumple it up and throw it into the back of your mind, shake it off and forget about it.

Upon waking, be very careful and lie still. Don't open your eyes too fast, and do your best to remember everything about the dream and write it all down quickly. If it doesn't come to you that night, don't worry, the Dream Maker will help you. Repeat the process until you have the answer.

When interpreting the dreams, you can also ask yourself the question: How does this dream provide a solution to my problem? The answer will come. When using dreams to solve a problem, make sure to write out the problem/challenge at the top of the page when recording your dream and see how it pertains to the issue you need to solve.

The Movie Theatre

Watch the dream as if it were on a movie screen in your mind's eye. Imagine you are in your own personal movie theatre and watching your Dream on a screen. Start the movie where the Dream left off when you woke up, let it play out, and finish through free flow. If there are things left undone, let it play out on the screen for you to understand. Then record it.

The Body's Dreaming

The body is like the physical alchemical vessel, and it is the space that contains the psychic fluid of your unconscious and your dream work. Learning to check in with your body during your dreaming practice is integral to your journey and something to incorporate as you continue this great work.

During dream interpretation, learning to work with the body is diving into unspoken feelings, emotions, and sensed perceptions.

When talking about our dreams, we tend almost to forget our bodies. Since the dream can seem to be a solely mental undertaking, we are creating an alchemical container within your psyche and your body to let new psychic energies come in and change our lives.

The Dreambody is an experience that Arnold Mindell identified in the late 1970's. What he saw was a sensed connection between our nightly dreams and our body experiences.

Bring Your Body Into Your Dreamwork With These Six Steps

- Begin by finding your center.
- Can you get a sense of what is unclear in the moment? What is arising from the dream in your body?
- What memories, images, and sensations are coming up from the unclear you are exploring right now?
- Can you stay with it and return to it again?
- How does the body want to express itself in this moment?
- Work with the movement, and repeat the actions until some clarity is reached.

Other questions to ask

- Is something in the dream an analogy for the body?
- How does the dream want to act in your body?
- What actions do you want to take when working with the dream?
- What messages are coming up through the actions?
- How do you want to move when exploring the dream?

- When talking about the dream, what is going on in the body?
- What can you sense is arising in your body?

Chakra Dreaming

Your dreams can also sometimes be connected to your chakras, and the blockages or opportunities for growth can be revealed. The chakras have corresponding elements and colors, and if they appear in your dream, play around with them and see if those colors match a related chakra. Is there an issue in a region where a chakra is located? Has a chakra been mentioned? Are there particular elements or colors that are associated with the chakra? It would be beneficial to get curious about any blockages that might hinder or prevent your personal growth.

Chakra Elements

- Root Chakra (Muladhara) - Groundedness, Earth Element, Red, Ruby
- Sacral Chakra (Svadhishthana) - Life Force Energy, Water Element, Orange, Carnelian
- Solar Plexus Chakra (Manipura) - The Personal Will, Fire Element, Yellow, Citrine
- Heart Chakra (Anahata) - Emotions & Feeling, Air Element, Green, Emerald
- Throat Chakra (Vishuddha) - Creative Expression, Sound Element, Aquamarine
- Third Eye Chakra (Ajna) - Intuition, Light Element, Dark Blue/Purple, Amethyst
- Crown Chakra (Sahasrara) - Connection to Source, Thought Element, Violet/ White, Quartz

- Root Chakra - Age of Development 1-7 years old
- Sacral Chakra - Age of Development 8-14 years old

- Solar Plexus - Age of Development 15 - 21 years old
- Heart Chakra - Age of Development 22 - 28 years old
- Throat Chakra - Age of Development 29 - 35 years old
- Third Eye - Age of Development 36-42 years old
- Crown Chakra - Age of Development 43-49 years old

If you did find a corresponding chakra dream. How did the experiences of this age shape your life and its effect on the particular chakra? Remember to take it easy on yourself. Dreamwork can be pretty challenging, overwhelming, and exhausting.

Dream Gestalt Exercise

This exercise usually encourages the dreamer to use active imagination to re-experience the dream through memory and imagination, often from the point of view of some other dream character or element than the dream ego.

In this process, the therapist would ask the dreamer to write down everything they remember from the dream. The dreamer is then encouraged to act out each part of the dream and create a conversation between the characters. For example, if a person dreams of a woman standing in the forest, the dreamer would be instructed to ask the woman questions. The dreamer could ask numerous questions to the dream figure and answer back as her. This back and forth dialogue can help clarify the dream message and progress the therapeutic process.

Start A Dream Group

Find a group of people interested in doing dreamwork and meet with them at least once a week. Everybody shares their dreams, and as a community, they help each other work on their dreams. People who usually create dreaming groups are caring, compassionate, and aware people.

The dream group is almost like a magic circle or a trusted community. Feel free to use the other exercises as a community to help each other interpret your dreams.

Caduceus with the Sun and Moon.

Dream Herbs

"Because the dream never tells you what you know already. It always points to something you don't know, a blind spot"
— Marie-Louise Von Franz:
The Way Of The Dream.

At one time, folk healers from around the globe worked with herbs to help them dream and receive insights. Medicine people were able to identify different herbs around their villages and in the forest that would aid in dreaming. There are many different plants that could be mentioned in this book, but for the sake of simplicity, three have been provided: a dream herb from Mexico known as Calea zacatechichi, another from Africa called Silene undulata, and the witch's herb from Europe, Mugwort. These plants have been used for thousands of years to aid with the practice of dreaming.

These plants are known today as oneirogens, which derives from the greek word óneiros, meaning "dream" and gen, which means "to create." These plants have been known to induce different states of sleep like rapid eye movement (REM) and hypnagogia, to name a few. They also aid in lucid dreaming and out-of-body-experiences (OBE). There is much that you can learn regarding the use of herbs and dreaming. You can make teas and tinctures — you can even smoke them. There are complex alchemical methods for extracting things from plants. For the sake of this book, the herbs discussed can easily be made into teas.

The following pages will describe each herb, where it comes from, and how to prepare it for use. Make sure to do your research and consult a health professional if you feel unsure of working with these plants.

Calea Zacatechichi (Mexico) — For Vivid Dreams and Lucid Dreaming

Calea Zacatechichi is a dreaming herb primarily used by the Chontal people in Oaxaca, Mexico. They call it thle-pela-kano, which means "leaf of God." They will use it when they need to know the cause of an illness or a lost person's location. The plant's ritual use is to smoke it while drinking its tea and then immediately lie down to sleep. You will know it has worked once you feel peacefulness, drowsiness, and begin to hear your heartbeat.

Instructions for use:
1. Take 2-3 grams and steep it in water for 15 minutes.
2. Roll another gram into a cigarette.

3. While it is steeping, concentrate on what you want Calea to teach you, and then after it has steeped, drink the tea, and then smoke the cigarette while lying down. You should feel drowsy.
4. Upon waking, write down your dream.

It is also useful for obtaining lucid dreams. Calea intensifies the vividness of the dream, so becoming lucid will be more likely. If you would like to use it to help with lucid dreaming, use it every night for two weeks.

Silene Undulata (South Africa) — For Prophetic Dreams

They are primarily used by the Xhosa people in Cape Town, South Africa. It is not the flower but the root that is said to induce dreams.

Instructions for use:

Method 1 (Morning): Mix half a teaspoon with a half cup of water and then drink it when you wake up in the morning while the stomach is empty. Eat food when you are feeling hungry.

Method 2 (Evening):

1. Mix a heaping teaspoon with half a liter of water.
2. Blend in the water until it gets frothy.
3. Suck the foam out of the container until you feel bloated and then fall asleep.

Important info: Make sure to ingest on an empty stomach; the alkaloids need time to travel through your system.

Before falling asleep, focus on the question you need to be answered.

Make sure to use the recommended amounts only. The recommended doses work, and more significant amounts will have a purging effect. There are no fatal or harmful side effects that have been reported.

The Xhosa shamans have said that using this plant was part of the "white magic path," and it is said to provide dreams from your ancestors, particularly from your paternal grandfather and great-grandfather. Dreaming is deeply embedded in the Xhosa culture, and they view dreaming as a gift from their ancestors, or the white winds.

Mugwort (Europe) — Visionary Herb and Lucid Dreaming

Primarily used by witches in Anglo Saxon Europe. Witches have used mugwort for centuries, and its use is found regularly in pagan magickal practices. They used it to burn as incense, cure illnesses, for shellwork, and other rituals.

Instructions for use:

Drink as a tea. It is best to drink 30-60 minutes before bed. It requires you to stay hydrated, so make sure you stay hydrated, or you may get some stomach aches when you take it.

The recommended dose is between 100-400 mg steeped in water. Try adding some honey to the tea for a better taste.

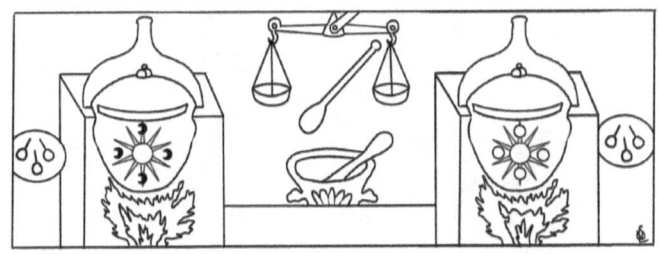

Moon and Sun Furnaces, showing the conjunction,
the union of opposites.

Bringing Awareness To Your Process

Dreamwork is a culmination of consistent practice and understanding the mythology underneath your conscious awareness. You can do this by saving some space at the end of your dream journal and making notes of repetitive people, animals, and current energies during this moment of your life. By discovering your dream community, you will find the collective psychic energy currently acting in your life. This is an important part of the dreamwork process. By reading through your journal and making notes of the different animals, landscapes, clothes, shadow figures, and your Anima/Animus, you will begin to experience a shift in your consciousness.

This is not by any means a quick and easy process. It will happen little by little and span the entirety of your life. But, it is valuable to your personal growth. By doing this work, you will find a river of new growth flowing right underneath your nose. The shadow issues and strengths, the Anima/Animus that gets projected onto the opposite sex and/or potential mates, and the ultimate Self, your true north star, guiding you to who you really are. This is you, what is happening within you. It is a puzzle that is slowly starting to put itself together.

Follow the exercises laid out in the following pages and see for yourself with your notes. Enjoy the wonder and the mystery that is your own unique process.

I love the story of Doubting Thomas. He's the one who is usually discredited in the Bible for doubting Jesus, the man who did not have faith. He was the only person who was allowed to see and touch the wounds of Jesus. He was the only one who asked questions and wanted to investigate. For that, he got the answers that he was seeking.

I invite you to be curious and challenge yourself during these fact-finding missions into the interior of your own unconscious. Discover your psychic landscape and layout the plan for your path for personal growth. It is a unique path, and it doesn't belong to anybody but you. I strongly recommend that you also work with a Jungian Analyst during this process, or at least somebody who respects dreams enough to help you understand what is happening. Dreams are dynamite material, and they need to be treated with the utmost respect.

> *"The most terrifying thing is to accept ourselves completely."*
> *- Carl Jung*

10 Dreams to Finding the Complex

- Take your last ten written dreams.
- Put the problem of each dream around a circle.
- Take the main issue(s) of the dream, and put it in the circle's center.
- This is the complex that the psyche wants you to work on right now.
- Try to interrelate the problems and solutions in the dreams.
- It might not be comfortable, but you will discover something illuminating.

Center Conflict

Inner Dream Community

The recurring characters in your dream series represent your current complexes and archetypal patterns and can sometimes shed light on a future psychological direction. They will define what is currently happening psychologically in your life right now.

Outline all your inner dream community members at the end of your completed dream journal. They can be people, animals, plants, mythological creatures, etc. Whatever beings continue to appear in your dreams. Identify the top five that are consistently reoccurring, and then answer your inner dream community questions in the following pages. List each dream character's associations, mythological associations, personality traits, etc. Then write whatever comes to mind for the free flow description. Do this for each dream character, and then answer the reflection questions at the end.

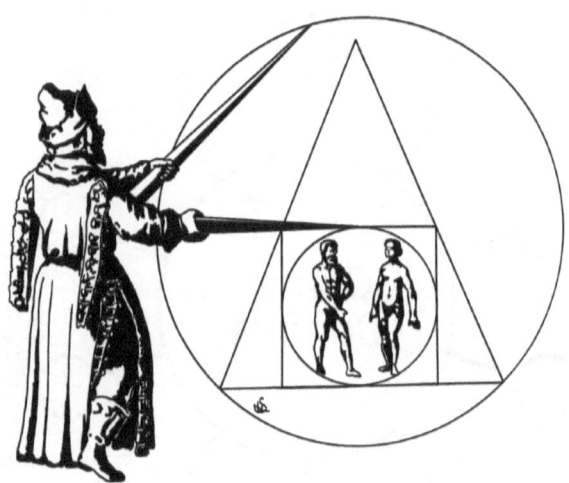

The Philosopher's Stone

#1
....
What Archetype (if any) is this?

....
What are the main associations & energies that you have with this character?

-
....
-
....
-
....
-
....
-
....
-
....

How does the energy of this dream character show up in your psyche and how does it relate to your life right now?

....

....

....

....

....

....

....

#2

....

What Archetype (if any) is this?

....

What are the main associations & energies that you have with this character?

- ....
- ....
- ....
- ....
- ....
- ....

How does the energy of this dream character show up in your psyche and how does it relate to your life right now?

....

....

....

....

....

....

....

#3

....

What Archetype (if any) is this?

....

What are the main associations & energies that you have with this character?

- ....
- ....
- ....
- ....
- ....
- ....

How does the energy of this dream character show up in your psyche and how does it relate to your life right now?

....

....

....

....

....

....

....

#4

....

What Archetype (if any) is this?

....

What are the main associations & energies that you have with this character?

- ....
- ....
- ....
- ....
- ....
- ....

How does the energy of this dream character show up in your psyche and how does it relate to your life right now?

....

....

....

....

....

....

....

#5
....

What Archetype (if any) is this?

....

What are the main associations & energies that you have with this character?

- ....
- ....
- ....
- ....
- ....
- ....

How does the energy of this dream character show up in your psyche and how does it relate to your life right now?

....

....

....

....

....

....

....

Inner Dream Community Reflections

What kind of energy does your Inner Dream Community have?

....

....

....

....

....

How do you think this community is showing up in your life?

....

....

....

....

....

....

....

....

....

Inner Animals

Animals represent your instinctual drive and your animal tendencies. They can express how you instinctually move and behave in the world.

Outline all animals you have seen in your dreams at the end of your completed dream journal. Identify the top five consistently reoccurring animals, and then answer the questions about your inner animals and instinctive psychic energy in the following pages. For each animal in your top five list, write about the key traits of the animal that resonate with you. Then write about how the animal is mythologically portrayed, and then reflect and write about these traits and how they relate to your instincts. Once each animal has been worked through, answer the reflection questions at the end.

Green Lion Eats The Sun

#1

What are some key traits of this animal?

-
-
-
-
-

Mythologically, how is this animal portrayed?

How does this relate to your instincts?

#2

What are some key traits of this animal?

- ....
- ....
- ....
- ....
- ....

Mythologically, how is this animal portrayed?

....

....

....

....

How does this relate to your instincts?

....

....

....

....

....

....

#3

What are some key traits of this animal?

- ....
- ....
- ....
- ....
- ....

Mythologically, how is this animal portrayed?

....

....

....

....

How does this relate to your instincts?

....

....

....

....

....

....

#4

What are some key traits of this animal?

- ....
- ....
- ....
- ....
- ....

Mythologically, how is this animal portrayed?

....

....

....

....

How does this relate to your instincts?

....

....

....

....

....

....

#5

What are some key traits of this animal?

- ....
- ....
- ....
- ....
- ....

Mythologically, how is this animal portrayed?

....

....

....

....

How does this relate to your instincts?

....

....

....

....

....

....

Inner Animal Reflections

Which animal resonates with you the most and why?

....

....

....

....

....

How can you use your inner instinctual drive to aid you in your life?

....

....

....

....

What similarities do you notice about your inner animals and how you act in the world?

....

....

....

....

Inner Landscapes

Our inner landscapes are the setting of the dramatic structure of our dreams. They are also where our unconscious can be currently "placed" or is situated.

Outline all the locations where your dream takes place at the end of your completed dream journal. Identify your associations to these places and why your unconscious is set here. Identify the top five consistently reoccurring locations, and then answer the questions in the following pages. After these five places have been answered, answer the questions in the provided reflection questions.

Splendor Solis

Mark Gowland • **Dream Speak**

#1
....
What are your main associations and/or memories of this place?

- ....
- ....
- ....
- ....
- ....
- ....
- ....

Why or how do you think your unconscious is set here?

....

....

....

....

....

....

....

....

#2

....

What are your main associations and/or memories of this place?

- ....
- ....
- ....
- ....
- ....
- ....
- ....

Why or how do you think your unconscious is set here?

....

....

....

....

....

....

....

....

#3

What are your main associations and/or memories of this place?

-
-
-
-
-
-
-

Why or how do you think your unconscious is set here?

#4

What are your main associations and/or memories of this place?

-
-
-
-
-
-
-

Why or how do you think your unconscious is set here?

Mark Gowland • **Dream Speak**

#5
....

What are your main associations and/or memories of this place?

- ....
- ....
- ....
- ....
- ....
- ....
- ....

Why or how do you think your unconscious is set here?

....

....

....

....

....

....

....

....

Inner Landscape Reflections

How do these places relate to the setting of your unconscious?

....

....

....

....

....

....

....

What kind of influence does this have on your life?

....

....

....

....

....

....

....

Dream Ego

Identifying key behaviors from your Dream Ego will help you understand how you act and behave in your life. It will help you identify helpful and unhelpful behaviors, or your "fallback" unconscious behaviors in your daily life.

Outline all the repeating actions or behaviors you are doing in your dreams. Identify the top five actions or behaviors reoccurring at the end of your completed dream journal. Then answer the questions on the following pages. Identify the core associations that you understand about your behaviors, and then write a free flow description of these behaviors and why you are doing them. Then write about if this behavior is helping or hindering you in life. After these five actions or behaviors have been answered. Answer the Dream Ego Reflection questions.

The Labyrinth

#1

What are the reasons you behave this way?

- ....
- ....
- ....
- ....

Free Flow Description about this behaviour

....

....

....

....

Does this behaviour help or hinder you in life?

....

....

....

....

....

....

....

#2

What are the reasons you behave this way?

- ....
- ....
- ....
- ....

Free Flow Description about this behaviour

....

....

....

....

Does this behaviour help or hinder you in life?

....

....

....

....

....

....

#3

What are the reasons you behave this way?

- ....
- ....
- ....
- ....

Free Flow Description about this behaviour

....

....

....

....

Does this behaviour help or hinder you in life?

....

....

....

....

....

....

#4

What are the reasons you behave this way?

- ....
- ....
- ....
- ....

Free Flow Description about this behaviour

....

....

....

....

Does this behaviour help or hinder you in life?

....

....

....

....

....

....

....

#5

What are the reasons you behave this way?

- ....
- ....
- ....
- ....

Free Flow Description about this behaviour

....

....

....

....

Does this behaviour help or hinder you in life?

....

....

....

....

....

....

....

Dream Ego Reflections

What behaviours do you what to change and why?

....

....

....

....

....

....

....

What are more empowering behaviours that you can make?

....

....

....

....

....

....

....

Persona

The persona is revealed in dreams by the clothes presented to you the dreamer, what you are wearing, or clothes that stand out to you.

Outline all the articles of clothing that stand out in your dreams at the end of your completed dream journal. Identify the top five persona clothes that are consistently reoccurring and then answer the questions in the following pages. Then write whatever comes to mind for the free flow description, then answer the question of how this persona role is presenting itself in your life and if it is helping or hindering you in your life. After these five articles of clothing have been worked through, get to know your persona and answer the reflection questions at the end.

The Mask of Loki

#1

What type of person wears this type of clothing?

- ....
- ....
- ....
- ....

Free Flow Description

....

....

....

....

How does this relate to your Persona?

....

....

....

....

....

....

....

#2

What type of person wears this type of clothing?

-
-
-
-

Free Flow Description

How does this relate to your Persona?

#3

What type of person wears this type of clothing?

- ....
- ....
- ....
- ....

Free Flow Description

....

....

....

....

How does this relate to your Persona?

....

....

....

....

....

....

....

#4
....
What type of person wears this type of clothing?

-
....
-
....
-
....
-
....

Free Flow Description

....

....

....

....

How does this relate to your Persona?

....

....

....

....

....

....

....

#5

What type of person wears this type of clothing?

- ....
- ....
- ....
- ....

Free Flow Description

....

....

....

....

How does this relate to your Persona?

....

....

....

....

....

....

....

Persona Reflections

What have I started to notice about the clothing in my dreaming?

....
....
....
....
....
....
....
....

Do I identify too much with this Persona?

....
....
....
....
....
....
....

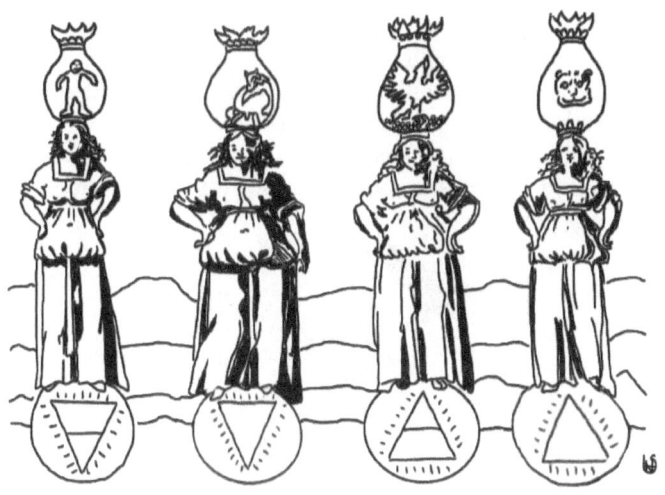

Four stages of the Alchemical Process

Discover Your Shadow

Understanding your shadow drives is an integral part of your process. The shadow is a part of your personality that you have repressed and have deemed not acceptable traits to present in your life.

Outline all the people in your dreams who are of the same sex as you and of relatively similar age at the end of your completed dream journal. Identify the top five shadow characters in the frequency of appearance. Then answer the questions in the following pages, describe the key personality traits of the shadow character, write a free flow description of your associations with that shadow character, and answer the question "how does this relate to your shadow?" After each shadow character has been finalized, begin to meet your shadow and answer the reflection questions at the end.

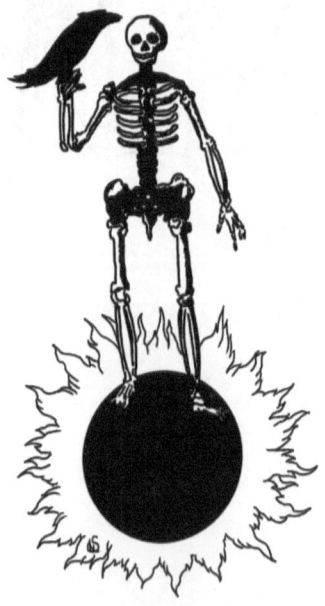

Putrefactio - Sol Niger

#1

Key Personality Traits

- ……………………………………………………………………
- ……………………………………………………………………
- ……………………………………………………………………
- ……………………………………………………………………

Free Flow Description

……………………………………………………………………

……………………………………………………………………

……………………………………………………………………

……………………………………………………………………

What do you understand about your Shadow?

……………………………………………………………………

……………………………………………………………………

……………………………………………………………………

……………………………………………………………………

……………………………………………………………………

……………………………………………………………………

……………………………………………………………………

#2

Key Personality Traits

-
-
-
-

Free Flow Description

What do you understand about your Shadow?

#3

Key Personality Traits

- ....
- ....
- ....
- ....

Free Flow Description

....

....

....

....

What do you understand about your Shadow?

....

....

....

....

....

....

....

#4

Key Personality Traits

- ....
- ....
- ....
- ....

Free Flow Description

....

....

....

....

What do you understand about your Shadow?

....

....

....

....

....

....

....

#5

Key Personality Traits

-
-
-
-

Free Flow Description

What do you understand about your Shadow?

Shadow Reflections

Recurring Shadow Emotions, Actions, Situations, and Personality Traits:

- ....
- ....
- ....
- ....

Describe your Shadow

....

....

....

....

How can you integrate your Shadow in a positive way?

....

....

....

....

....

....

Meet Your Anima/Animus

Meeting and encountering your contra sexual half is a more advanced form of dreamwork. If you are really committed to doing this work, you will eventually have to work with a Jungian Analyst to help you understand and identify your Anima or Animus.

Take note of all the contrasexual people you do not recognize and the contrasexual symbols in your dreams. Identify the top five contrasexual energies in the order of frequency of appearance. Then answer the questions in the following pages, describe each image's key traits, and then a free flow description of each image, and meditate on how this gets projected onto the opposite sex. After each contrasexual character is worked through, answer the reflection questions at the end..

Figura Quatra - Philosopha Hermitca

#1

Key Personality Traits

- ....
- ....
- ....
- ....

Free Flow Description

....

....

....

....

....

How does this get projected onto the opposite sex?

....

....

....

....

....

....

#2
....
Key Personality Traits

- ....
- ....
- ....
- ....

Free Flow Description

....

....

....

....

....

How does this get projected onto the opposite sex?

....

....

....

....

....

....

#3

Key Personality Traits

- ...
- ...
- ...
- ...

Free Flow Description

How does this get projected onto the opposite sex?

#4

Key Personality Traits

-
-
-
-

Free Flow Description

How does this get projected onto the opposite sex?

#5

Key Personality Traits

- ....
- ....
- ....
- ....

Free Flow Description

....

....

....

....

....

How does this get projected onto the opposite sex?

....

....

....

....

....

....

Anima/Animus Reflections

Now, review and read through these interactions.

How do you think this affects your relationships with the opposite sex?

....

....

....

....

....

....

How does your Anima/Animus affect your life?

....

....

....

....

....

....

....

....

What is your Anima / Animus Teaching you?

....

....

....

....

....

....

....

Where is your Animus / Anima Hindering You?

....

....

....

....

....

....

....

....

Your Process

After reviewing all your dreams, and finishing all the reflections. It is time to ask yourself some real questions.

What are you starting to notice about your process?

....

....

....

....

....

....

....

How can you embody these lessons into your daily life?

....

....

....

....

....

....

....

What kind of ritual can you perform to honour your process?

A Final Word

Dream Speak is a meat and potatoes introduction to dream analysis and interpretation. It is not necessarily the full scope of the art form.

I have attempted to introduce you to the art of dreaming and give you a tool to empower your own life, a life where you live authentically, creatively, and in alignment with your dreaming power.

Doing this work will stop you from looking outward for guidance and start receiving it from within. This work will uncover many personal obstacles, memories, and wishes you have forgotten or are just vaguely aware of.

It is important to remember that working with a Jungian analyst is imperative while doing this kind of work, especially when you take it seriously. Dream Speak is not a run of the mill dream dictionary; this is dynamite material that you are unearthing. It is a powerful and dynamic art form that must be handled with care. There is no doubt that sensitive and deeply personal information will emerge from this type of work. It can be unsettling, emotional, confusing, and powerful.

Like most people venturing out into the backcountry, you will need a guide. A guide keeps you safe, leads you based on your risk tolerance, and can help you through your individuation process.

Learning to work with dreams is very interesting, and when teamed up with a trained Jungian analyst, it becomes a vessel for emotional transformation.

I genuinely hope that this has provided some value for you and your life journey. Life is a sacred act, and it goes by too fast. None of us can escape the fact that this life will end, and it is uncertain what lies beyond that veil. But in the process of living, from now until that time we pass on to the great beyond, I hope you can live close to your dreaming power, awaken to the beautiful possibility that is your life, and that you never stop exploring. Remember that you can continue to grow as long as you live.

It has been an honor.

"Golden flower"

Bibliography

Jung, Carl G. *The Undiscovered Self.* Princeton NJ Princeton University Press 2011

Jung, Carl G. *Dreams.* Princeton NJ: Princeton University Press 2011

Jung, Carl G. *Man And His Symbols,* New York, NY, Doubleday, 1964

Jung, Carl G. *Dream Analysis Part 1,* England, Routledge, 1995

Johnson, Robert A. *Inner Work: Using Dreams and Active Imagination for Personal Growth.* New York: HarperCollins 1986

Johnson, Robert A. *Understanding the Dark Side of the Psyche.* New York: HarperCollins

Mindell, Arnold. *The Dreammakers Apprentice.* Charlottesville VA: Hampton Roads Publishing Company 2001

Whitmont, Edward C. *Dreams, A Portal To The Source.* New York: Routledge 1989

Matoon, Mary Ann. *Understanding Dreams.* Dallas TX: Spring Publications 1984

Jung, Emma. *Animus And Anima.* Putnam CT: Spring Publications 1985

Kalsched, Donald. *The Inner World of Trauma: Archetypal Defences of the Personal Spirit.* New York: Routledge 2010.

Gendlin, Eugene T. *Let Your Body Interpret Your Dreams.* Wilmette, IL: Chiron Publications, 1986

Mindell, Arnold. *Working with the Dreaming Body.* Portland, OR: CreateSpace Independent Publishing Platform 2014

Mindell, Arnold. *Dreambody: The Body's Role In Revealing The Self.* Santa Monica CA: SIGO PRESS 1982

Stein, Murray. *Jung's Map Of The Soul: An Introduction.* Peru, Illinois: Open Court Publishing Company 2010

Castleman, Tess. *Sacred Dream Circles: A Guide to Facilitating Jungian Dream Groups.* Einsiedelen, Switzerland: Daimon Verlag 2009

Castaneda, Carlos. *The Art of Dreaming.* New York City, NY: William Morrow Paperbacks 2003

Waggoner, Robert. *Lucid Dreaming: Gateway to the Inner Self.* Needham, MA: Moment Point Press 2009

Norbu, Namkhai. *Dream Yoga and the Practice of Natural Light.* Ithica. NY: Snow Lion Publications 2002

Boa, Fraser. *The Way of the Dream*, Toronto, Windrose Films Ltd 1988

Chögyal Namkhai Norbu. *Dream Yoga and the Practice of Natural Light,* Ithaca, NY, Snow Lion Publications, 1992

Mindell, Arnold, *The Dreammaker's Apprentice,* Charlottesville, VA Hampton Roads Publishing Company, 2001

Bhatnagar, Sri Shyamji, Microchakras, InnerTuning For Psychological Well-being, Rochester, Vermont, Inner Traditions, 2009

Lectures

Singer, June. *The Art of Dreaming: Living The Creative Life.* Chicago, IL: CG Jung Institute of Chicago 1998

Khan, Lois. *Typical Dream Imagery.* Chicago, IL: CG Jung Institute of Chicago 1986

Lavin, Thomas Patrick. *Dream Interpretation and Amplification.* Chicago, IL: CG Jung Institute of Chicago 1986

Stein, Murray. *The Big Dream.* Chicago, IL: CG Jung Institute of Chicago 1986

Schwartz-Salan, Nathan. *The Myth of Shadow and the Shadow of Myth.* Chicago, IL: CG Jung Institute of Chicago 1991

Bolen, Jean Shinoda. *The Wounding Shadow of the Wounded Healer: Narcissism and Co-Dependency in the Helping Professions.* Chicago, IL: CG Jung Institute of Chicago 1991

Stein, Murray. *Jung's Concept of the Anima.* Chicago, IL: CG Jung Institute of Chicago 1989

Kalschand, Donald PhD. *Dream Imagery Constellated by the Analytic Process.* Chicago, IL: CG Jung Institute of Chicago 1989

Klein, Lucielle. *Jung's Concept of the Animus,* Chicago, IL: CG Jung Institute of Chicago 1991

Khan, Lois. *Animus Images in Dreams, Myths, and Fairytales,* Chicago, IL: CG Jung Institute of Chicago 1991

Wiedemann, Florence and Polly Young-Eisendrath, *Female Authority,* Chicago, IL: CG Jung Institute of Chicago 1989

Stevens, Caroline. *Animus as Servant to the Self,* Chicago, IL: CG Jung Institute of Chicago 1989

Wyly, James. *Anima & Animus,* Chicago, IL: CG Jung Institute of Chicago 1994

Research Papers

Effects of Vitamin B6 (Pyridoxine) and a B Complex Preparation on Dreaming and Sleep
Denholm J. Aspy, Natasha A. Madden, Paul Delfabbro

https://journals.sagepub.com/doi/full/10.1177/0031512518770326

Jung, Carl G. *On The Method of Dream Interpretation: Seminar 1.* Princeton, NJ: Princeton University Press : http://assets.press.princeton.edu/chapters/s8500.pdf
Hoffman, Curtiss Dumuzi's Dream: Dream Analysis in Ancient Mesopotamia, Educational Publishing Foundation 2004

Websites For Further Reference

CG Jung Institute Of Chicago: www.jungchicago.org

World of Lucid Dreaming: https://www.world-of-lucid-dreaming.com/

Dreamwork Psychology: www.dreamwork-psychology.com

www.ingramcontent.com/pod-product-compliance
Lightning Source LLC
Chambersburg PA
CBHW030220170426
43194CB00007BA/801